BEYOND ALFALFA SPROUTS & CHEESE

The Healthy Meatless Cookbook

Judy Gilliard & Joy Kirkpatrick, R.D.

Library of Congress Cataloging-in-Publication Data

Gilliard, Judy,
    Beyond Alfalfa Sprouts and Cheese: The Healthy
    Meatless Cookbook / by Judy Gilliard
    and Joy Kirkpatrick.
            p.   cm.
    Includes Index
    ISBN 1-56561-020-2 $12.95
    1. Vegetarian cookery. I. Kirkpatrick, Joy.
        II. Title.
    RM236.G55   1993
    641.5'636--dc20   93-16904
                                            CIP

Edited by: Donna Hoel
Cover Photo: Anthony Blake/Tony Stone Images
Cover Design: Terry Dugan
Interior Design: Liana Raudys
Production: Claire Lewis
Printed in the United States of America

10 9 8 7 6 5 4 3 2

Published by: CHRONIMED Publishing
P.O. Box 47945
Minneapolis, MN 55447-9727

◆ Dedication ◆

This book is dedicated to everyone
pursuing a health-conscious lifestyle.

◆ Acknowledgements ◆

For support and inspiration: Jeanne Jones, Amanda and
Ron Roisum, Chef Patricia Hook and Gregory Hook,
Wendy Dunson, Nancy Anderson, Dick and Gloria
Schroeder, Janet Feltenberger, John and Pat Borer, Pete
and Linda Spiers, Jim and Leann Rogers, Milt and Sandra
Levinson, the Edgars, the Gilliards, the Schweits, the
Hardacres, and the Izens.

To David Wexler, David Unruh, Jon Ebersole, Donna
Hoel, and the rest of the talented staff at CHRONIMED
Publishing for their help in creating this book.

To Bruce Good, Patricia Roberts, and Chef Dimitri
Mainos at the Royal Cruise Line for continuous support.

To Naomi Guttman and Roberta Urich for their contin-
ued assistance and knowledge of nutritional analysis.

To Sheila Cluff, Mark Joseph, and Chef Raymond at The
Palms at Palm Springs.

To Ralph's Grocery Company and Jensen's of Palm
Springs—a shopper's delight.

Finally, extra special thanks to: Nicole Virgilio for
sharing her mom, Mona, with us for days and days;
Neoma Ray for hours of figures and numbers; Teri
Gilliard for fabulous illustrations—again; Eleanor
Kirkpatrick for dusting off her typewriter and spending
hours typing recipes; and Jan Mazza for her fast fingers
and fine eye.

◆ Our Taste Testers ◆

Eleanor Kirkpatrick, George Lanning, Rod Murphy, Kathy and David Middleton, Tom and Mona Virgilio, Frank and Michelle DiPietro, Jan and Denny Mazza, and Jan and Harvy Izen.

◆ Table of Contents ◆

◆ Preface ◆

With three GUILTLESS GOURMET cookbooks behind us, Joy and I were anxious to get started on our fourth. Then our publisher, David Wexler, asked us to hold off—he was busy researching some ideas in areas that are often lacking in health-conscious cookbooks. About a month later, he suggested our next book be on vegetarian cooking. He asked for a book not necessarily only for the vegetarian, but also for those who want to start incorporating more vegetarian meals in their food plans. This idea was exciting to Joy and me. We have had an interest in learning more about vegetarian cooking. After all, it's low in fat and calories, is created mostly from fresh ingredients, and has lots of flavor. And, of course, preparing vegetarian meals can be quick and easy.

A lot of people today are cutting back on animal protein in their meal plans, and there's a large variety of wonderful vegetarian food on the market. Also, many restaurants now offer good vegetarian alternatives, other than just steamed rice and vegetables. There is actually no end to the great tasting and healthy dishes that you can prepare without meat. We chose to incorporate dairy foods in our recipe development, but if you don't eat dairy, these recipes can be altered by using soy milk and soy cheese as substitutes.

In developing our recipes, we definitely kept in mind the busy working woman—or working man—with ideas on how to prepare meals that are quick and easy, tasty and yet healthy. Some items are easily frozen, and others will hold well for several days in the refrigerator.

One of the key things we have learned while developing health-conscious recipes is the importance of using fresh or very high-quality ingredients. That's what keeps flavor at its peak, so that's what we recommend. We also hope that using our book will inspire you to use your creativity in developing your own meal plans and revising your favorite recipes to make them more healthful.

While I was on a cruise recently, I was delighted to spend some time with the head chef of Greek Royal Cruise Lines, Chef Dimitri Mainos. The time spent in his kitchen gave me great ideas for meal planning. At the beginning of each day he prepares a basic tomato sauce, from which he can create many other sauces. By making a large pot of basic sauce and freezing it in small portions, we can also have a sauce that will be ready at all times.

Making the change to a more health-conscious lifestyle is becoming easier. Restauranteurs and hoteliers are much more sensitive to the needs of the public today than they were in the '80s. You can turn any restaurant into a health-conscious restaurant just by ordering carefully.

For example, order your salad dressing on the side, or order just a cruet of vinegar, or lemon wedges. The majority of fat is hidden in the dressing. Order your meat broiled or grilled. If the meal includes sauces, ask for them on the side. If the menu offers chicken picata or fish with a butter-picata sauce, ask instead for yours to be broiled with fresh lemon juice and capers without the butter. Most good restaurants will gladly do this today. Their aim is to please the customer. The same is true of hotels. More and more are offering spa cuisine or heart-healthy cuisine, featuring items approved by the American Heart Association.

The most important thing in changing to a more health-conscious lifestyle is to plan ahead: By taking the time to think through the changes you are making, you can be prepared. Remember, change is difficult. But eventually the change becomes a habit—second nature. That's how you're going to maintain your weight. Be careful not to fall back into old habits.

Grocery stores are making it easier, too, by offering a wide variety of fat-free items: fat-free sour cream, fat-free cottage cheese, and even several reduced-fat cheeses are now on the market. Be sure not to purchase items that are fat-free just because they are zero-fat. Make sure you like them—if you don't, you may rebel and revert to old habits. Keep tasting to find those items you truly enjoy. Always buy new products in the smallest container, just in case.

Set up your kitchen to be more health-conscious. Take one morning and completely clean out your kitchen cupboards. Throw out all the old spices. Remember, they only have a shelf life of one year—two if they are kept in the refrigerator. Stale spices and herbs will give your food a stale taste. Buy spices in the smallest container available. Before adding herbs or spices to food, grind them with a mortar and pestle to release their flavor. Using fresh herbs adds a lighter, more mellow flavor. Fresh herbs are available today in many markets, or grow them in your garden or window box. Prepare fresh herbs ahead of time by cleaning, drying, chopping, placing them in a freezer bag, and storing them in the freezer. They will keep for about six weeks. Fresh parsley should always be kept in the freezer, ready for use, since it is much better than the dried variety. For easy access, keep it in an airtight container.

Throw out all the old items that are stuck way in the back of the cupboard. Throw out all the items that are high in fat. If they are canned products, and they are still good, give them to a food drive. Don't keep things that are not included in your new lifestyle. Reorganize everything so that it is easy and fun to use.

Go through and check on your different containers— loaf pans, tureens, casserole dishes. Make a list of kitchen utensils you would like to have or that you need for your new style of cooking. It's very important to have the right equipment. It makes it a lot easier in preparation, and it is more fun to serve. There are many items on the market, from classic French White Corningware® to exotic oven-to-table potteries. When you are buying equipment or new items for your kitchen, be sure they make life easier and still present a beautiful table.

Judy Gilliard
Joy Kirkpatrick

◆ Foreword ◆

We would like to highlight three products you will see used in this book.

Butter Buds™

We are very fond of this product and have used it in all our books. It can be used in its dry form to sprinkle on hot, moist foods. However, for cooking, we generally prefer using it in its liquid form (you add the water). It adds a nice flavor and contains no fat at all. Look for it in a bright yellow box in your grocery store—usually in the health food or diet section.

Kashi

Kashi is a terrific product that we personally use more than we have indicated in this book. Kashi is a tasty combination of grains available as two different types of products. In this book, we use the Kashi pilaf style that cooks like rice. It is also available as a puffed cereal. Both products are delicious, high in fiber, and low in calories. Kashi is available in the cereal section or health-food section of your grocery store. If you cannot locate it, you can buy it direct from a company called Deliteful Options—call 1-800-685-LITE. (See Kashi Stroganoff, pg. 125; and Kashi Nut Loaf, pg. 143.)

Wax Orchards

Wax Orchards products are of very high quality and taste. Their whole product line contains no added sugar, just what is found in the fruit itself. The Fudge Sweet is a chocolate lover's delight—and it's totally fat free. Look for Wax Orchards in specialty stores or order direct from Deliteful Options at 1-800-685-LITE. (See Raspberry Pudding Cheesecake, pg. 187, and Chocolate Cheesecake, pg. 188.)

◆ Introduction ◆

Who is a Guiltless Gourmet?

Definition: *Guiltless* - innocent or without guilt

Definition: *Gourmet* - an expert judge of good food and wine

We are often asked why we are Guiltless Gourmets. To some, the two words are diametric opposites. How can one be a gourmet and still be guiltless? The dictionary definition answers the question. Too often we think of a gourmet as an individual who, with nose in the air, barks orders to a waiter and pays a high price for a small portion of very rich food. Instead, quality, taste, and presentation are the hallmarks of today's Guiltless Gourmets. Chefs across the country are learning and teaching new techniques of food preparation based on diners' desires for quality food with low-fat content. Freshness of ingredients, ease of preparation, and attractive presentation form today's trend in fine dining.

The authors are both health conscious, aware, and always looking for ways to develop a recipe with an eye for less fat, but still plenty of flavor. In addition, the recipe must be easy to prepare, using a minimum of ingredients. Further, we need to be able to buy those ingredients at a local grocery store.

We think a Guiltless Gourmet meal might look like this:

California Citrus Salad (pg. 72)
with Citrus Herb Dressing (pg. 82)
41 calories

Spaghetti with Fresh Basil and Pine Nuts
(pg. 136)
255 calories

Raspberry Pudding Cheesecake (pg. 187)
158 calories

The color, the presentation, the ease of preparation, and the taste of this meal are classic Guiltless Gourmet. The calories total 454 with less than 10 grams of fat in the whole meal. Compare this with a meal of steak, baked potato with butter and sour cream, salad with dressing, and dessert—an average of 1500 calories and more than 60 grams of fat.

We encourage you to join us and become Guiltless Gourmets. Together we can enjoy life, the pleasure of dining on fine food, and ultimately a more health-conscious lifestyle.

Vegetarianism

We know of a prominent physician who stated many years ago that vegetarianism was just a fad. We believed he was wrong then and we're sure of it now. Vegetarianism is no passing fancy. We could write a history of vegetarianism, but this is not a history book, nor a novel. It's a cookbook. We will forego much ancient history and take a quick look at the twentieth century.

In the first half of this century, many thinkers espoused vegetarianism, for reasons that varied from religious concerns to health and lifestyle choices. Later, people such as Adelle Davis were very influential as the so-called "health foods" writers emerged. In those years, roughly in the 1950s, the science of nutrition was new, as was the massive refinement and processing of foods. At one point, in the 1970s, there was such a gap between those who espoused "health foods" and those who were into steaks and chops that another classic book was written: *Nuts Among the Berries*, by Ronald Deutsch. This book attempted to make some sense of the very different views and documentation of what food is good for us versus what may be harmful. Revised editions of this book are still available and still make valuable reading.

Perhaps the two classic books on vegetarianism are Frances Moore Lappe's *Diet for a Small Planet* and the ever-popular *Laurel's Kitchen* by Laurel Robertson and Carol Flinders. This book, subtitled *A Handbook for Vegetarian Cookery and Nutrition*, was first published in the '70s. It continues to be a very well-respected cookbook as well as a compendium of nutrition information.

As we began researching recipes and techniques for this book, it struck us that though many vegetarian recipes are free of animal products, they are by no means low or even controlled in fat. As we look to the '90s, we see that low-fat cooking is the trend and therefore, our challenge! Vegetarian recipes tend to be heavy in oils, nuts, seeds, cheese, and egg yolks. All healthy and nutritious foods to be sure, but nevertheless they are primarily fat. As we all struggle to reduce total fat to 30 percent or less in our diets, a healthy dose of olive oil or a generous handful of cheese can be our downfall.

Most people have their own personal definition as to what vegetarianism is. For many, simply not eating red meat means they are vegetarian. Others may eat fish, but no poultry or red meat. For clarification, we include here some simple definitions of the different types of vegetarianism:

> Lacto-ovo vegetarian: Allows milk, dairy products, and eggs.
>
> Lacto-vegetarian: Allows milk and dairy products.
>
> Vegan: A total vegetarian who eats only fruits, vegetables, grains, nuts, and seeds, and no milk, dairy products, or eggs.

To be sure, many people go through phases in their lives where they feel a change in their diet is in order. Often, vegetarianism is the type of change they look for. We strongly encourage you to talk this over with your physician and consult a dietitian if you really plan to pursue a change. As will any other lifestyle change, vegetarianism requires some study. Sufficient protein is essential; adequate calcium and total calories also need to be considered. If you're moving toward becoming a complete vegan, seek out a source for vitamin B12 as you can't obtain this vitamin in a diet totally free of meat and dairy foods. The bottom line is variety and' moderation. Eating six cups of brown rice a day or a large vegetable salad does not a healthy vegetarian make.

Is Tofu for You?

Most people have heard of it—though many have no idea what it is. Tofu is not a new invention. In fact, it has been a staple of some Asian populations for hundreds of years. Tofu is made from soy beans, and the finished product resembles a block of cheese or a baked custard. Tofu has very little flavor of its own; in fact, one of its virtues is that it picks up the flavors of the foods with which it is prepared.

Tofu is readily available in most grocery stores. You generally will find it in a refrigerated section of the store. It is packed fresh in water, which needs to be changed daily as you store the tofu in your refrigerator. It should be used within a few days. Tofu can be purchased in aseptic containers that require no refrigeration and have a much longer shelf life. It is usually labeled as soft, firm, or extra firm. The type you buy depends on what you plan to use it for. Soft tofu is great for shakes and items that do not require the tofu to hold its shape. Firmer varieties are best for use in dishes where you want to see the tofu in chunk form. The Tofu Stroganoff (pg. 94) and Broiled Tofu (pg. 173) are two examples. Draining tofu before using it in a recipe is often important. Simply place the tofu in a colander, cover it with a plate, then weigh it down with cans of food or other 1 to 2 pound objects. The longer the tofu drains (minutes to hours), the firmer it becomes.

The real virtue of tofu is its nutritional makeup. Following are some points you may want to consider as you become more familiar with tofu and its uses.

1. Tofu is high in protein but contains no animal products.

2. Tofu is low in fat and calories and contains no cholesterol. Four ounces of tofu contain about 2 grams of fat and 50 calories.

3. Tofu is quite high in calcium, making it an excellent source of a mineral that can be lacking in a vegetarian diet. Four ounces of tofu can provide over 100 mg. of calcium.

4. Tofu is a very inexpensive protein source with hundreds of uses in cooking.

The '90s ... Taking Control of the Fat

The '90s have brought a new awareness of the bad
effects a high-fat diet can have on your life. The basic
fact is that fat is what makes you fat. By taking fat out of
your diet, you will live a healthier and happier life. By
learning to cook with less fat and learning to eat smart
when you eat away from home, you can maintain the
weight you desire without ever having to go on another
diet! Also, by cooking with less fat, you are reducing
calories so you end up getting more nutrition in the
calories you consume.

Carbohydrates and protein contain 4 calories per gram,
while fat at 9 calories per gram contains more than
double. One ounce of protein contains 7 grams.
However, most proteins also contain some fats, so one
ounce of lean meat would also contain 3 grams of fat.

Keep in mind that change is always difficult at first.
However, once you learn to balance for fat intake, it
becomes easy and fun because the end results are so
positive.

Remember to set up your kitchen for lower fat cooking.
Take the time to get rid of items in your cupboards that
are old or that contain fat. Take the low or nonfat route
in the supermarket. For example, watch out for fats:

> 8 oz. whole milk = 160 calories with 8 gm. fat
>   or 45 percent of calories from fat.

8 oz. low-fat milk 2% = 140 calories with 5 gm. fat
or 32 percent of calories from fat.

8 oz. low-fat milk 1% = 120 calories with 2 gm. fat
or 15 percent of calories from fat.

8 oz. nonfat milk = 80 calories with 0 gm. fat
and no calories from fat.

8 oz. evaporated skimmed milk = 200 calories with
0 fat and no calories from fat.

Increase your use of whole grains, cereals, rice, and flours. Keep fresh fruits and vegetables around. Always have apples on hand. Prunes also are a great source of fiber and sweetness, and they add moisture.

Here are the foods you can substitute to reduce fats:

Original food	Substitute
Milk or cream	Nonfat, 1%, or evaporated milk
Butter	Butter Buds™ or Molly McButter™
Cheese	Low-fat cheese
Eggs	1 egg = 2 egg whites
Mayonnaise	Buy reduced-fat variety
Sour cream	Reduced-fat or plain nonfat yogurt
Sauté foods	Reduced chicken broth, non-stick sprays (Pam™), or olive oil
High-fat dips	Yogurt cheese, whipped nonfat cottage cheese, reduced-fat sour cream

To figure your daily maximum amount of fat grams:

Multiply your desired weight by 10. This is the number of calories you need to consume daily to maintain that weight. Add 20 percent to that to allow for moderate exercise. Take 30 percent of that number and you will have the number of fat calories you need. Divide that by 9 to arrive at the number of grams of fat you can eat in a day to maintain your ideal weight. (No, you cannot save them up!)

For example:

If you weigh 140 pounds, multiply by 10 for 1400 calories. Add 20 percent for exercise and you get 1680 calories to maintain a weight of 140 pounds. Thirty percent of 1680 calories is 504 that can come from fat. Divide that by 9 and you get 56 grams of fat as your daily maximum. If you keep your fat grams to 40, you can eat 144 calories more in nonfat foods.

Plan Ahead

Plan your meals and snacks; be prepared with protein bars, dry low-fat cereal, dried fruit, and nonfat salad dressing in your desk drawer at work or in your hand-bag. On days when you have the time, prepare extra food and freeze it. Or if you plan to eat it in a few days, keep it in airtight containers in your refrigerator.

Remember, fat is what makes you fat. Try to keep your
fat intake to 40 grams or less per day. Most of all, make
yourself feel good. If you feel good, you will look
good, and you will be a good example to everyone
around you.

In 1971, Finland had the highest rate of death from
heart disease. The Finnish government launched a
massive educational campaign centered around eliminating unnecessary fat from the diet. By 1991, the
country of Finland had climbed from the bottom of the
statistical pile to ranking the ninth healthiest in the
world. In the U.S., heart disease is the number one
health problem. In Greece and Italy, the incidence of
heart disease is very low. These populations consume a
lot of vegetables, breads, and pasta. Their main source
of fat is olive oil. We can learn from them.

◆◆◆

Breakfast Bounty

◆◆◆

◆ Breakfast in a Bowl ◆

2 cups nonfat cottage cheese
1/4 cup nonfat sour cream
1 T. fructose
1 tsp. lemon juice
1 T. lemon zest
1/8 tsp. nutmeg
2 cups fresh fruit, cut up, or 2 small
   cantaloupes, cut in half and seeded
1 cup Guiltless Granola (see pg. 16)

1. Combine first six ingredients and blend well.
2. Divide fresh fruit into 4 bowls. Top with 1/4 of the cottage cheese mixture, then with 1/4 cup Guiltless Granola. If using small cantaloupes, fill center of melon with cottage cheese mixture, then top with Guiltless Granola.

Makes 4 servings.

Each serving contains:
222 calories, 17 gm. protein, 25 gm. carbohydrate, 7 gm. fat,
27 mg. sodium, 11 mg. cholesterol,
3 gm. fiber

ADA Exchange Value
1/2 Bread, 1 Fruit, 2 Lean Meat
27% of total calories are from fat

◆ Blueberry Pancakes with Blueberry Sauce ◆

1 cup flour
1/2 tsp. baking soda
1/2 tsp. baking powder
2 T. corn oil margarine
2 egg whites
1 whole egg
1 1/2 cups buttermilk
1 cup fresh or frozen blueberries

1. Combine flour, baking soda and baking powder in a bowl. Cut in margarine.

2. In another bowl, combine egg whites, egg and buttermilk.

3. Add egg mixture to flour and stir just to combine.

Gently fold in blueberries.

4. Bake on preheated griddle.

Makes 15 pancakes. 1 serving = 3 pancakes

Each serving contains:
169 calories, 6 gm. protein, 23 gm. carbohydrate,
5 gm. fat, 301 mg. sodium,
3 mg. cholesterol, 1 gm. fiber

ADA Exchange Value
1 Bread, 1/2 Fruit, 1 Fat
29% of total calories are from fat

◆ Blueberry Sauce ◆

2 T. fructose
2 T. cornstarch
1/2 cup water
1 cup fresh or frozen blueberries

Combine first three ingredients in a pan. Add berries. Bring to a boil and cook until thickened and clear.

Makes 1 cup. 1 serving = 2 T.

Each serving contains:
22 calories, <1 gm. protein, 5 gm.
carbohydrate, <1 gm. fat, 4 mg. sodium,
0 cholesterol, <1 gm. fiber

ADA Exchange Value
1/3 Fruit
Negligible percentage of total calories are from fat

♦ Guiltless Granola ♦

2 cups rolled oats
1/4 cup wheat germ
2 large shredded wheat biscuits,
   crumbled
2 T. slivered almonds
1/4 cup assorted dried fruit
1 T. oil
1/4 tsp. cinnamon
1 tsp. vanilla
2 dates
2 T. baby food plums
1 egg white

1. Mix all ingredients together.
2. Bake at 300 degrees for 45 minutes, stirring every 15 minutes.
3. Cool, then store in an air-tight container.

Makes 3 cups. 1 serving = 1/2 cup.

Each serving contains:
196 calories, 7 gm. protein, 30 gm. carbohydrate, 6 gm. fat,
10 mg. sodium, 0 cholesterol, 3 gm. fiber

ADA Exchange Value
1 Bread, 1 Fat, 1 Low-fat Meat
28% of total calories are from fat

◆ Bran Muffins ◆

1 cup oat bran
1 cup whole wheat pastry flour
1 T. fructose
1 1/2 tsp. baking soda
4 egg whites
1 1/2 cup low-fat buttermilk
1/4 cup molasses

1. Preheat oven to 350 degrees.
2. Combine oat bran, flour, fructose, and baking soda in a bowl.
3. Mix egg whites, buttermilk, and molasses together.
4. Stir liquid mixture into flour mixture enough to moisten.
5. Pour batter into 12 paper-lined muffin tins or tins sprayed with a nonstick spray.
6. Bake for 25 minutes. Let cool.

Makes 12 muffins.

Each serving contains:
100 calories, 5 gm. protein, 18 gm. carbohydrate,
1 gm. fat, 193 mg. sodium, 1 mg. cholesterol, 1 gm. fiber

ADA Exchange Value
1 Bread
9% of total calories are from fat

◆ Raspberry Corn Muffins ◆

1 cup yellow corn meal
1 cup whole wheat pastry flour
1 T. baking powder
1 cup low-fat buttermilk
3 egg whites
1 T. fructose
3/4 cup raspberries, fresh or frozen,
    unsweetened

1. Preheat oven to 400 degrees.

2. Combine corn meal, flour, and baking powder in a large mixing bowl.

3. Combine buttermilk, egg whites, and fructose. Mix well.

4. Add liquid mixture to dry mixture. Blend well.

5. Spray 12 muffin tins with nonstick spray or line with paper cups. Fill each 1/4 full.

6. Place 3 raspberries in the center of each and top with remaining batter.

7. Bake 20 minutes until golden brown.

Makes 12 muffins.

Each serving contains:
92 calories , 3 gm. protein, 19 gm. carbohydrate, <1 gm. fat, 134 mg. sodium, <1 mg. cholesterol, 1 gm. fiber

ADA Exchange Value
1 Bread
<4% of total calories are from fat

◆ Carrot Prune Muffins ◆

1/3 cup fructose
1/4 cup molasses
4 egg whites
1 cup grated carrots
1 cup pitted, chopped prunes
1/4 cup low-fat buttermilk
1 cup oat flour
1/2 cup unprocessed bran
1 cup whole wheat pastry flour
2 tsp. baking powder
1 tsp. ground cinnamon
1/2 tsp. nutmeg
1/4 tsp. ground ginger
1/4 tsp. ground cloves
1/4 tsp. baking soda
1/2 cup chopped walnuts

1. Preheat oven to 350 degrees.
2. Mix together fructose, molasses, egg whites, carrots, prunes, and buttermilk.
3. Mix together all dry ingredients. Combine with liquid mixture and blend well.
4. Spray 12 muffin tins with nonstick spray. Pour batter in equal amounts into tins and bake 25 minutes.
5. Let stand 15 minutes before removing from tins.

Makes 12 muffins.

Each muffin contains:
159 calories, 5 gm. protein, 29 gm. carbohydrate, 3 gm. fat,
126 mg. sodium, <1 mg. cholesterol, 3 gm. fiber

ADA Exchange Value
2 Bread, 1/2 Fat,
17% of total calories are from fat

◆ Oatmeal Breakfast Bars ◆

1/2 cup fructose
8 egg whites
1 cup nonfat milk
2 T. molasses
2 1/2 tsp. vanilla
1 T. dry Butter Buds
1 cup whole wheat pastry flour
1 cup oat bran
3 cups rolled oats
1 tsp. baking powder
2 tsp. cinnamon
1 cup raisins

1. Preheat oven to 350 degrees.
2. Mix fructose, egg whites, milk, molasses, vanilla, and Butter Buds together. Blend well.
3. Mix together flour, oat bran, rolled oats, baking powder, cinnamon, and raisins.
4. Stir liquid mixture into flour mixture and mix well.
5. Spray a 9" x 13" baking pan with a nonstick spray. Pour batter into pan and bake 15 minutes. Cool and cut into 16 bars.

Each bar contains:
116 calories, 5 gm. protein, 21 gm. carbohydrate, 1 gm. fat,
124 mg. sodium, <1 mg. cholesterol, 1 gm. fiber

ADA Exchange Value
1 1/2 Bread,
7% of total calories are from fat

◆ Apple Walnut Muffins ◆

3/4 cup unbleached flour
3/4 cup whole wheat pastry flour
1/4 cup oat bran
2 1/2 tsp. baking powder
1 tsp. cinnamon
1/4 tsp. nutmeg
4 egg whites
2/3 cup apple juice concentrate
1 large apple, cored, and chopped
1/2 cup chopped walnuts

1. Preheat oven to 400 degrees.
2. Mix all dry ingredients in food processor or blender.
3. Mix together egg whites, apple juice, apple, and walnuts.
4. Stir together liquid mixture and dry mixture until moistened.
5. Spray 12 muffin tins with nonstick spray or line with paper cups. Fill with equal amounts of batter.
6. Bake 20 minutes.

Makes 12 muffins.

Each muffin contains:
111 calories, 4 gm. protein, 17 gm. carbohydrate, 3 gm. fat,
100 mg. sodium, 0 cholesterol, 1 gm. fiber

ADA Exchange Value
1 1/2 Bread, 1/2 Fat
24% of total calories are from fat

◆ Peanut Butter Breakfast Bars ◆

These bars are excellent for breakfast on the run. Kids love
them. The bars are high in fat but worth the splurge.

> 16 oz. jar of unsalted, natural-style nutty
>   peanut butter, with 1/4 cup oil poured
>   off the top
> 1/2 cup fructose
> 2 T. molasses
> 6 egg whites, slightly beaten
> 1 T. Butter Buds
> 2 tsp. vanilla
> 1 cup nonfat milk
> 1/2 cup oat flour
> 1/2 cup whole wheat flour
> 1 cup oat bran
> 3 cups rolled oats

1. Preheat oven to 350 degrees.

2. Cream together peanut butter, fructose, and
molasses.

3. Add egg whites, Butter Buds, vanilla, and milk.

4. Slowly add flours, oat bran, and rolled oats. Mix
well.

5. Put mixture in a 9" x 13" pan sprayed with
nonstick spray.

6. Bake 15 minutes. Cool. Cut into 16 bars. Wrap
in foil and keep in refrigerator.

◆ ◆ ◆

Makes 16 bars.

Each bar contains:
275 calories, 14 gm. protein, 26 gm. carbohydrate, 14 gm. fat,
124 mg. sodium, <1 mg. cholesterol, 4 gm. fiber

ADA Exchange Value
1 Bread, 1 Fruit, 3 Fat
46% of total calories are from fat

◆ French Toast ◆

2 whole eggs
4 egg whites
1/4 cup nonfat milk
1 tsp. vanilla
1/4 tsp. nutmeg
1 tsp. cinnamon
8 slices French or sourdough bread

1. Mix together all ingredients except bread, in a flat-bottomed bowl that will hold a single slice of bread.

2. Dip each slice of bread into egg mixture, making sure to saturate well.

3. Brown bread in a large skillet sprayed with non-stick coating.

Makes 4 servings.

Each serving contains:
155 calories, 10 gm. protein, 19 gm. carbohydrate, 4 gm. fat,
267 mg. sodium, 137 mg. cholesterol,
1 gm. fiber

ADA Exchange Value
1 Bread, 1 Lean Meat
23% of total calories are from fat

Beyond Alfalfa Sprouts & Cheese

◆ Granola Yogurt Pancakes ◆

5 T. flour
3 T. Guiltless Granola (pg. 16)
1 tsp. fructose
1 tsp. baking soda
4 egg whites
1/2 cup Yogurt Cheese (pg. 177)

1. Spray griddle, crepe pan, or other nonstick skillet with nonstick spray. Preheat pan so that a small drop of water "dances" when it hits the surface.

2. Combine flour, granola, fructose, and baking soda.

3. Stir egg whites into yogurt cheese with a whisk until smooth. Stir in flour mixture lightly to maintain the lightness of the egg whites.

4. Using about 2 T. of batter per pancake, bake until lightly browned on one side, then carefully turn and bake until done.

Makes 8 pancakes. 1 serving = 2 pancakes

Each serving contains:
98 calories, 8 gm. protein, 14 gm. carbohydrate, <1 gm. fat,
372 mg. sodium, 4 mg. cholesterol, >1 gm. fiber

ADA Exchange Value
1 Bread
12% of total calories are from fat

◆ Orange Cheese Spread ◆

Use on toast, crackers, muffins or bagels.

3 T. low-sugar orange marmalade
1 cup nonfat cottage cheese
2 T. fat-free sour cream
1 T. orange zest, finely grated

Combine all ingredients and mix well. Allow to stand several hours to bring out the flavor.

Makes 1 1/2 cups. One serving = 2 T.

Each serving contains:
24 calories, 2 gm. protein, 3 gm. carbohydrate, <1 gm. fat,
4 mg. sodium, 1 mg. cholesterol, 0 fiber

ADA Exchange Value
1/2 Lean Meat
<10% of total calories are from fat

◆ Breakfast Bread from the Bread Machine ◆

A nice feature of these bread-machine recipes is that you can put your breakfast bread in the bread maker the night before and awaken to the smells of homemade bread. Or, you can set the timer so homemade bread will be ready when dinner is ready.

1 cup whole wheat pastry flour
1/2 cup oat flour
1/2 cup oatmeal
1 tsp. Butter Buds
1/2 cup raisins
1/2 cup walnuts
2 T. fructose
2 T. molasses
1/2 tsp. cinnamon
7/8 cup water
1 pkg. dry yeast

Make the bread according to the directions on your machine. (Basically, that means putting everything in the machine and turning it on.) Makes a 1-pound loaf.

One-sixth of loaf contains:
183 calories, 5 gm. protein, 31 gm. carbohydrate, 5 gm. fat, 12 mg. sodium, 0 cholesterol, 3 gm. fiber

ADA Exchange Value
1 Bread, 1 Fruit, 1 Fat
25% of total calories are from fat

◆ Peasant Bread from the Bread Machine ◆

1 cup whole wheat pastry flour
1/2 cup brown rice flour
1/4 cup unbleached white flour
1/4 cup corn meal
1 tsp. Butter Buds
2 T. fructose
1 T. molasses
7/8 cup water
1 pkg. dry yeast.

Make according to the directions for your bread machine. Makes a 1-pound loaf.

One-sixth of loaf contains:
117 calories, 3 gm. protein, 26 gm. carbohydrate,
<1 gm. fat, 14 mg. sodium,
0 cholesterol, 1 gm. fiber

ADA Exchange Value
1 Bread, 1 Fruit,
<3% of total calories are from fat

◆ ◆ ◆

Appetizers

◆ ◆ ◆

◆ Eggplant Appetizer ◆

1 large eggplant, unpeeled unless skin is
 leathery, diced into 1/2-inch pieces
1 cup tomatoes, diced
2 T. tomato paste
2 cloves garlic, crushed
1 T. lemon juice
1 tsp. fructose
2 tsp. ground cumin
1 T. capers
1/4 tsp. cayenne pepper
1 cup water

1. In a large saucepan, bring water to a boil and
add eggplant. Cook over medium heat until tender.
Drain and mash.
2. Add rest of ingredients and combine well.
3. Chill several hours or overnight.
4. Serve as a garnish, relish, or with crackers or
bread as an appetizer.

Makes about 3 cups, or 12 servings.
1 serving = 1/4 cup.

Each serving contains:
11 calories, <1 gm. protein, 2 gm. carbohydrate, 0 fat,
97 mg. sodium, 0 cholesterol, <1 gm. fiber
ADA Exchange Value
Values negligible per serving

◆ Carrot Cheesecake Appetizer ◆

1 medium onion, chopped (a sweet onion
   is preferred)
2 cloves garlic, minced
2 cups carrots, grated
2 T. orange juice
2 T. fresh basil, minced, or 2 tsp. dried
2 T. fresh oregano, minced, or 2 tsp. dried
3/4 tsp. ground ginger
1 1/2 cups low-fat ricotta cheese
1/2 cup part skim mozzarella cheese,
   shredded
1/4 cup Parmesan cheese, grated
4 egg whites, lightly beaten

1. Spray large skillet with nonstick spray. Heat to medium and sauté onion and garlic until soft and translucent.

2. Add carrots, stir and sauté for 2 minutes.

3. Add orange juice, basil, oregano, and ginger. Remove from heat.

4. In a large bowl or food processor, combine the three cheeses and blend until smooth. Beat in egg whites until well combined.

5. Stir in carrot mixture.

6. Preheat oven to 375 degrees.

7. Spray a 6" spring-form pan with nonstick spray. Spoon cheese mixture into pan and smooth out.

8. Place in oven with pan of water on shelf below. Bake for 50 minutes or until top is browned and knife inserted in center comes out clean.

9. Turn off heat, open oven door, and let cheese-cake stand 15 minutes.

10. Remove from oven, cool for 20 minutes. Serve warm with bread or crackers, or chill for several hours before serving.

◆ ◆ ◆

Makes 24 servings.

Each serving contains:
41 calories, 3 gm. protein, 4 gm. carbohydrate, 2 gm. fat,
46 mg. sodium, 5 mg. cholesterol,
<1 gm. fiber

ADA Exchange Value
1 Vegetable, 1/2 Lean Meat
35% of total calories are from fat

◆ Bean Spread ◆

2 large cloves garlic, peeled
1/2 cup fresh basil leaves
1/2 cup fresh parsley
2 cups cooked white beans
Juice of one lemon
Fresh ground black pepper

1. Purée or process garlic, basil, and parsley in a blender or food processor.

2. Add beans and blend until smooth. Add lemon juice and ground black pepper to taste.

Makes 1 1/2 cups. 1 serving = 1 T.

Each serving contains:
19 calories, 1 gm. protein, 4 gm. carbohydrate, <1 gm. fat,
1 mg. sodium, 0 cholesterol, 1 gm. fiber

ADA Exchange Value
1/4 Bread
4% of total calories are from fat

◆ Black Bean Spread ◆

4 cups cooked black beans
1 cup medium hot salsa

Put beans and salsa in food processor and whip
with steel blade until pureed and smooth.

Makes 8 servings.

Each serving contains:

114 calories, 7 gm. protein, 22 gm. carbohydrate, 1 gm. fat,
15 mg. sodium, 0 cholesterol, 10 gm. fiber

ADA Exchange Value
1 1/2 Bread
8% of total calories are from fat

◆ Feta Spread ◆

8 oz. light cream cheese
7 1/2 oz. hoop cheese
3 oz. feta cheese

Put all ingredients in food processor and whip
with steel blade until smooth.

Makes 8 servings.

Each serving contains:
78 calories, 7 gm. protein, 2 gm. carbohydrate, 5 gm. fat,
206 mg. sodium, 10 mg. cholesterol, 0 fiber

ADA Exchange Value
1 Medium Fat Meat
58% of total calories are from fat

◆ Olive Pimento Spread ◆

7 oz. hoop cheese
12 small green olives, pitted
2 T. diced pimento

In the food processor, whip hoop cheese until smooth using steel blade. Add olives and pimento and pulse to blend.

Makes 8 servings.

Each serving contains:
24 calories, 3 gm. protein, <1 gm. carbohydrate, 1 gm. fat, 145 mg. sodium, 1 mg. cholesterol, <1 gm. fiber

ADA Exchange Value
1/2 Lean Meat
38% of total calories are from fat

◆ Spanish Cream Cheese Spread ◆

8 oz. light cream cheese
7 1/2 oz. hoop cheese
16 oz. jar chunky medium salsa
(drained in strainer)

1. In food processor, blend hoop cheese and cream cheese with steel blade until smooth and well mixed.
2. Add salsa and pulse until well blended.

Makes 8 servings.

Each serving contains:
71 calories, 5 gm. protein, 2 gm. carbohydrate, 5 gm. fat,
88 mg. sodium, 20 mg. cholesterol, <1 gm. fiber

ADA Exchange Value
1 Medium Fat Meat
63% of total calories are from fat

◆ Herbed Cottage Cheese ◆

Use on cucumber slices, bell pepper slices, or oatmeal
crackers (pg. 47). Delicious as a topper for baked
potatoes.

> 1 1/2 cups nonfat cottage cheese
> 1 clove garlic, pressed through a garlic
> press
> 1/2 tsp. caraway seeds
> 1 tsp. fresh dill weed
> 2 tsp. fresh parsley, minced, or 1 tsp. dried
> 2 tsp. fresh basil, minced, or 1 tsp. dried
> 2 T. lemon juice
> Fresh ground black pepper

Combine all ingredients and mix well.

Makes 1 1/2 cups or 6 servings. 1 serving = 1/4 cup.

Each serving contains:
32 calories, 6 gm. protein, 1 gm. carbohydrate, <1 gm. fat,
6 mg. sodium, 3 mg. cholesterol, 0 fiber

ADA Exchange Value
1 Lean Meat
6% of total calories are from fat

◆ Spinach Paté ◆

2 boxes frozen spinach, thawed and
    drained
1 small onion, minced
2 cloves garlic, minced
2 tsp. fresh thyme or 1 tsp. dried
2 tsp. fresh oregano or 1 tsp. dried
1 T. wine vinegar
6 egg whites
1/2 cup 1% milk
1/8 tsp. nutmeg
1/4 cup parsley, chopped
1/2 cup low-fat Swiss cheese, grated
3/4 cup whole wheat bread crumbs
Fresh ground black pepper

1. Preheat oven to 350 degrees.

2. Spray loaf pan or paté terrine with nonstick
spray, line with waxed paper, then spray waxed paper
lightly.

3. Squeeze moisture out of spinach, then chop very
fine.

4. Spray a large skillet with nonstick spray. Heat to
medium, then sauté onion and garlic until tender. Add
spinach, thyme, oregano, and vinegar. Stir to blend
well and cook about 5 minutes. Remove from heat.

5. In a large bowl, combine egg whites with milk and stir in spinach. Stir in nutmeg, parsley, grated cheese, bread crumbs, and pepper.

6. Pour mixture into loaf pan or terrine. Smooth top and cover with a piece of waxed paper sprayed with nonstick spray. Cover pan with foil or lid and bake for 45 minutes or until the top begins to brown.

7. Remove from oven, cool, and unmold.

Serve on Oatmeal Crackers (pg. 47) or as a side dish with a dollop of Basic Tomato Sauce (pg. 169).

Makes 24 slices.

Each slice contains:
63 calories, 6 gm. protein, 8 gm. carbohydrate, 1 gm. fat,
108 mg. sodium, 3 mg. cholesterol, 3 gm. fiber

ADA Exchange Value
1 Vegetable, 1 Lean Meat
14% of total calories are from fat

◆ Guacamole ◆

7 1/2 oz. hoop cheese
2 medium avocados
1/4 cup salsa

1. Put hoop cheese in food processor and whip with steel blade until smooth.
2. Add avocado and salsa and blend well.

Makes 8 servings.

Each serving contains:
104 calories, 5 gm. protein, 6 gm. carbohydrate, 8 gm. fat, 11 mg. sodium, 1 mg. cholesterol, 2 gm. fiber

ADA Exchange Value
1 Vegetable, 1 1/2 Fat
70% of total calories are from fat

◆ Bean Paté ◆

6 cups cooked navy beans
1 medium onion, chopped
2 cloves garlic, minced
2 cups grated carrots
1/4 cup chopped parsley
6 egg whites, beaten
1 cup 1% milk
1 tsp. herb blend
8 oz. crumbled feta cheese
1/2 tsp. white pepper

1. Purée beans in food processor.
2. Sauté onion and garlic until soft in skillet sprayed with nonstick spray.
3. Put onions and garlic in food processor along with beans. Add remaining ingredients and puree everything together until they are very well mixed.
4. Pour into casserole dish, cover, and bake at 350 degrees for one hour.
5. Serve warm or cold with crackers.

Makes 12 servings.
Each serving contains:
173 calories, 12 gm. protein, 22 gm. carbohydrate, 5 gm. fat,
277 mg. sodium, 18 mg. cholesterol, 4 gm. fiber
ADA Exchange Value
1 1/2 Bread, 1 Lean Meat
26% of total calories are from fat

◆ Cheese Crackers ◆

1 1/4 cup all purpose flour,
1/4 cup wheat germ
2 tsp. celery seed
3/4 cup nonfat cottage cheese
3 T. oil

1. Stir together flour, wheat germ, and celery seed.

2. Add cottage cheese and oil. Stir until well blended.

3. Make into a tube-shaped piece of dough, wrap in plastic wrap, and chill for 1 to 2 hours.

4. Preheat oven to 450 degrees.

5. On a well-floured board or pastry cloth, roll 1/2 of the dough to about 1/8" thick. Cut with a 2" cookie cutter and place cracker rounds on a cookie sheet that has been sprayed with nonstick spray. Repeat with remaining dough.

6. Pierce each cracker with a fork 3 or 4 times. Place in 450-degree oven, then lower heat to 400 degrees.

7. Bake 12 to 15 minutes or until lightly browned. Remove from baking pan and cool on a rack.

Makes 40 crackers. 1 serving = 4 crackers
Each serving contains:
104 calories, 4 gm. protein, 12 gm. carbohydrate, 5 gm. fat,
2 mg. sodium, 1 mg. cholesterol, 1 gm. fiber
ADA Exchange Value
1 Bread, 1 Fat
39% of total calories are from fat

◆ Oatmeal Crackers ◆

1 1/4 cups old fashioned rolled oats
1/4 cup water

1. Preheat oven to 275 degrees.
2. Stir together 1 cup oats with water until dough forms a mass and stays together.
3. Sprinkle a board or pastry cloth with 2 T. oats. Place dough on top. With a rolling pin, roll dough to 1/8". Use rest of oatmeal as needed to prevent sticking.
4. Trim edges and cut dough in half. Lift dough to an ungreased cookie sheet. Use a knife to score dough into 1 1/2" squares without cutting all the way through.
5. Bake for 30 minutes; turn crackers over and bake 15 to 20 minutes more. Remove to a cooling rack. When cool, break into individual crackers.

Makes 20 crackers. 1 serving = 4 crackers.

Each serving contains:
77 calories, 3 gm. protein, 13 gm. carbohydrate, 1 gm. fat, negligible sodium, 0 cholesterol, 1 gm. fiber

ADA Exchange Value
1 Bread
15% of total calories are from fat

◆ Cheese Wafers ◆

1/2 lb. low-fat cheese, shredded
4 oz. Neufchatel cheese
1 cup flour
1/2 tsp. cayenne pepper
2 cups cornflakes, crushed

1. Preheat oven to 350 degrees.
2. Combine cheeses, flour, and cayenne pepper, and mix well.
3. Stir in cornflakes and shape into small balls about the size of a small walnut, then flatten with the palm of your hand. Roll out and cut into diamond shapes.
4. Place wafers on ungreased cookie sheets and bake 25 minutes. Remove and cool on racks.

Makes 40 wafers. 4 wafers = 1 serving.

Each serving contains:
151 calories, 8 gm. protein. 15 gm. carbohydrate, 6 gm. fat, 151 mg. sodium, 22 mg. cholesterol, <1 gm. fiber

ADA Exchange Value
1 Bread, 1 Fat
38% of total calories are from fat

◆ Striped Vegetable Tureen ◆

1 lb. medium carrots, scrubbed and cut
  into cubes with 1/2 T. dill weed
1/2 lb. yellow split peas, dried, with 1/2
  tsp. white ground pepper
10 oz. frozen chopped spinach, thawed
6 egg whites
1/2 tsp. nutmeg
Ground black pepper

1. Preheat oven to 325 degrees. Spray a 1-lb. loaf
pan with nonstick spray. Cut a strip of wax paper to
cover the bottom and up over the edge of each side.
Spray paper ith nonstick spray.

2. Cook carrots, peas, and spinach all in separate
pans until well done.

3. Drain each vegetable thoroughly and purée
separately in a blender or food processor, adding 2 egg
whites to each mixture. Season all three to taste with
black pepper. Add a little nutmeg to the spinach.

4. Spoon the carrot mixture into the loaf pan first,
leveling top with a spoon to make it even. Carefully
layer peas on top and smooth it out. Then add the
spinach on top.

5. Cover with foil and bake 45 minutes. Remove
foil and bake an additional 15 minutes. Remove from
oven and let cool. Then chill in refrigerator.

6. Cut in 10 slices and arrange on serving plate.

◆ ◆ ◆

Makes 10 servings.

Each serving contains:
48 calories, 5 gm. protein, 8 gm. carbohydrate, <1 gm. fat,
57 mg. sodium, 0. cholesterol, 2 gm. fiber

ADA Exchange Valu
2 Vegetable
3% of total calories are from fat

♦♦♦

Savory Soups

♦♦♦

◆ Herb Seasoning for Soup ◆

Use this as a completely salt-free seasoning for beans or rice. We like to add one whole recipe to a pot of beans as it adds delicious flavor and color.

1 tsp. paprika
1/2 tsp. celery seed
1/2 tsp. turmeric
2 tsp. thyme leaves
2 tsp. sage leaves
1 tsp. marjoram leaves
2 tsp. oregano leaves
1/2 T. ground black pepper
1/4 tsp. cayenne pepper

Combine all ingredients and crush with a mortar and pestle.

Calories are negligible

◆ Vegetable Stock ◆

4 onions, chopped
4 cloves garlic, chopped
2 leeks, cleaned and chopped
4 large carrots, peeled and chopped into
    large pieces
6 stalks celery with leaves, chopped
3 parsnips or turnips, cleaned and chopped
6 mushrooms, cleaned and chopped
1/2 bunch parsley, washed
4 medium tomatoes, washed and chopped
2 tsp. fresh thyme, chopped or 1 tsp. dried
2 tsp. fresh oregano, chopped
2 fresh sage leaves, or 1/4 tsp. dried sage
4 bay leaves
6 peppercorns, lightly crushed
6 quarts water

1. Spray bottom of large kettle with nonstick spray. Using medium heat, cook onions, leeks, and garlic for 5 minutes. Add carrots, celery, parsley, and mushrooms. Cook 3 to 5 minutes.

2. Add rest of ingredients. Heat to a boil, then reduce heat to low. Simmer partly covered until liquid is reduced by about half.

3. Strain, cool, and freeze into one-quart portions or in ice cube trays for a quick flavor addition to vegetables and sauces.

◆ ◆ ◆

Makes about 2 quarts. 1 serving = 1 cup

Each cup contains:
33 calories, 1 gm. protein, 7 gm. carbohydrate, <1 gm. fat,
30 mg. sodium, 0 cholesterol, <1 gm. fiber

ADA Exchange Value
1 Vegetable
0 calories are from fat

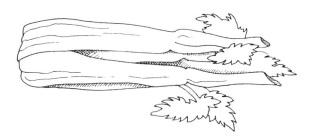

◆ Broccoli Potato Soup ◆

2 cups (about 3/4 lb.) broccoli florets
1 small onion, chopped
2 cloves garlic, minced
3/4 tsp. paprika
4 medium red potatoes, washed and diced
2 cups water
2 cups 1% milk
Fresh ground black pepper
1/4 cup fresh parsley, chopped
1/4 cup Parmesan cheese, freshly grated

1. Set aside 6 broccoli florets. Steam to crisp-tender, then plunge into cold water to retain green color.

2. Spray bottom of heavy soup kettle with nonstick spray. Heat to medium and sauté onion and garlic until tender.

3. Add paprika, broccoli, potatoes, and two cups of water. Bring to a boil, reduce heat, and simmer for 15 to 20 minutes, or until vegetables are soft. Cool slightly.

4. Blend or purée vegetable mixture and return to pot. Stir in milk, black pepper, and parsley. Heat, but do not boil.

5. Serve in soup bowls garnished with broccoli florets and Parmesan cheese.

Makes 6 servings. 1 serving = 1 cup.

Each serving contains:
97 calories, 6 gm. protein, 17 gm. carbohydrate, 1 gm. fat,
63 mg. sodium, 4 mg. cholesterol, 3 gm. fiber

ADA Exchange Value
1/2 Bread, 1/2 Nonfat Milk
10% of total calories are from fat

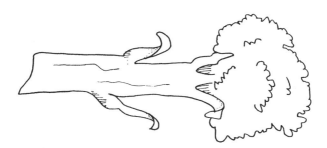

◆ Split Pea Soup ◆

1 lb. dried split peas
1 onion, chopped
3 carrots, peeled and chopped
3 stalks celery, chopped
1/2 cup fresh parsley, finely chopped
2 bay leaves
8 cups water or Vegetable Stock (pg.54)

1. Rinse and drain split peas, then put into a soup or crockpot.

2. Add rest of ingredients. If using a soup pot, bring to a boil, then cover and simmer 2 to 4 hours. If using a crockpot, turn on high heat for about an hour, then turn to low and simmer several hours.

Makes 8 servings.

Each serving contains:
191 calories, 14 gm. protein, 34 gm. carbohydrate, <1 gm. fat, 26 mg. sodium, 0 cholesterol, 7 gm. fiber

ADA Exchange Value
2 Bread
3% of total calories are from fat

◆ Dilled Zucchini Carrot Soup ◆

This can be served chilled with a dollop of yogurt, topped with fresh dill.

1 small onion, chopped
1 clove garlic, minced
2 cups zucchini, grated
1 cup carrots, grated
2 cups Vegetable Stock (pg. 54)
1 cup water
2 T. fresh dill, chopped, or 1 tsp. dried
2 T. lemon juice

1. Spray bottom of a heavy soup pot with nonstick spray. Using medium heat, sauté onion and garlic 1 to 2 minutes.

2. Add grated zucchini and carrots. Stir and sauté about one minute more.

3. Add vegetable stock, water, and one tablespoon of dill. Bring to a boil, reduce heat, cover and simmer about 10 minutes. Add lemon juice. Serve with remaining dill as a garnish.

◆ ◆ ◆

Makes 4 cups. 1 serving = 1 cup.
Each serving contains:
32 calories, 1 gm. protein, 7 gm. carbohydrate, <1 gm. fat, 10 mg. sodium, 0 cholesterol, 2 gm. fiber
ADA Exchange Value
1 1/2 Vegetable
8% of total calories are from fat

◆ Navy Bean and Tomato Soup ◆

1 T. olive oil
1 medium onion, chopped
1 cup carrots, chopped
1 cup celery, chopped
2 cups Basic Tomato Sauce (pg.169)
1 14-oz. can diced tomatoes in juice .
2 cups cooked navy beans (if using canned
   beans, rinse first)

1. Heat olive oil in a large Dutch oven. Add onions
and sauté until soft. Mix in carrots and celery.

2. Add beans, tomato sauce and diced tomatoes.
Cover and simmer for 1/2 hour.

Makes 8 servings.

Each serving contains:
93 calories, 5 gm. protein, 15 gm. carbohydrate, 2 gm. fat,
86 mg. sodium, 0 cholesterol, 3 gm. fiber

ADA Exchange Value
1 Bread
19% of total calories are from fat.

Satisfying Salads

♦♦♦

Exploring the Vegetarian Cuisine

As we enter the '90s, we are finding a new health awareness in the American public: watching fat intake in our diets; eating more complex carbohydrates; eating less animal protein. More people are choosing vegetarian cuisine. Since the 1960s we have learned a great deal about dietary fat. But eliminating animal fat and getting rid of cholesterol only takes care of part of the problem. Vegetable fats such as olive oil or corn oil still have just as many fat calories as animal fats, so it is important to watch the amount of vegetable fat you use in your diet and in cooking.

Most vegetables are very low in calories; you can eat a lot of vegetables and still maintain your weight. That is good news for those of us who need to watch what we eat and who want to keep ourselves fit at all times. To do this, we need to maintain balance in our meals. This means a balance in food groups: fruits, vegetables, breads, protein, and yes, even some fat.

If you are trying to lose weight, always keep an airtight container in your refrigerator filled with chopped vegetables in order to create salads. Here is a list of "free" vegetables and greens. "Free" means that each 1-cup size serving of these items raw is under 20 calories.

> Cabbage
> Celery
> Chinese cabbage

Cucumber
Green onion
Hot peppers
Mushrooms
Radishes
Zucchini
Endive
Escarole
Lettuce
Romaine
Spinach

If you wash the greens and spin them dry in a salad spinner, they will hold well in the refrigerator for four to five days.

You can create dozens of refreshing, filling salads, adding the different ingredients listed above to vary the tastes. A diced pear or an apple gives a fresh taste to a salad. Or you can add a cup of nonfat cottage cheese and toss it in with your dressing. Remember to use an oil-free dressing if you're watching out for extra calories. Use a fat-free dressing and add some nuts. Nuts are high in fat, but if you use no other fats, that's a good example of balancing. For extra protein, add any kind of beans—black beans, kidney beans, white beans, or blackeyes—that have been cooked. If you use canned beans, first rinse them in cold water to remove some of the sodium.

The following list gives you an idea of what your added
calories would be for each item added to your salad:

- 80 calories each: 1/3 cup beans, 1/2 cup corn,
  1/2 cup lima beans, 3 tablespoons grapenuts,
  1/2 cup peas

- 25 calories each: 1/2 cup cooked asparagus,
  1 cup raw bean sprouts, 1 cup raw carrots, 1 cup
  green peppers (raw), 1 large tomato, 1/2 cup
  cooked beets, 1 cup raw beets

- 60 calories each: 1 apple, 1 pear, 2 tablespoons
  raisins, 3/4 cup mandarin oranges

- 70 calories per 1/2 cup nonfat cottage cheese

- 55 calories per 1 oz. low-fat cheese, including
  Parmesan

- 45 (fat) calories each: 10 small olives, 2 whole
  walnuts, 6 dry roasted almonds, 1 tablespoon
  pine nuts or sunflower seeds (without shells),
  1/8 medium avocado, 2 tablespoons shredded
  coconut, 1 tablespoon of most regular salad
  dressings.

So have some fun and make those salads!

◆ "Great" Grated Carrot Salad ◆

1 1/2 lbs. carrots, peeled and grated
(about 4 cups)
2 T. chives, chopped
2 T. parsley, chopped
Juice of one lemon
1 T. balsamic vinegar
1 clove garlic, minced
2 tsp. Dijon-style mustard
1 T. olive oil

1. Combine carrots with parsley and chives.
2. Combine rest of ingredients, mix well, and toss
with carrots.

Makes 4 cups. 1 serving = 1/2 cup

Each serving contains:
25 calories, <1 gm. protein, 6 gm. carbohydrate, <1 gm. fat,
29 mg. sodium, 0 cholesterol, 1 gm. fiber

ADA Exchange Value
1 Vegetable
<7% of total calories are from fat

◆ Beet Salad ◆

1 lb. fresh beets, steamed until tender
2 T. fresh parsley, chopped or 1 T. dried
1 tsp. fresh dill, chopped or 1/2 tsp. dried
1/2 cup Yogurt Cheese (pg. 177)
1 clove garlic, put through a garlic press
1 tsp. caraway seeds, crushed
Fresh ground pepper
4 lettuce leaves

1. Cool beets, remove skins, and slice thin. Put into a glass or ceramic bowl. Add parsley and dill and mix carefully.

2. Combine Yogurt Cheese, garlic, caraway seeds, and fresh ground pepper. Toss carefully with beets and serve on a bed of lettuce.

Makes 3 cups. 1 serving = 1/2 cup

Each serving contains:
32 calories, 2 gm. protein, 6 gm. carbohydrate, <1 gm. fat,
42 mg. sodium, 1 mg cholesterol, 2 gm. fiber

ADA Exchange Value
1 Vegetable
<8% of total calories are from fat

◆ Rice Salad with Tofu and Vegetables ◆

1 cup zucchini, sliced
1/2 cup green beans, chopped coarsely
1/2 cup yellow crookneck squash, sliced
1/2 cup carrots, sliced
5 oz. tofu, drained and cut into cubes

1/2 cup jicama, chopped
1/4 cup red onion, chopped

3 cups cooked brown rice, chilled
1 cup nonfat sour cream
Juice of half a lemon
1 to 2 cloves garlic, minced

Dressing

1/4 cup red wine vinegar
1/4 tsp. dry mustard
1 T. olive oil
1/2 tsp. fresh dill
Fresh ground pepper

1. Steam zucchini, beans, squash, and carrots together for about 4 minutes. Plunge into cold water to stop cooking process and to retain color. Cool and drain.

2. Combine dressing ingredients, add jicama and onion. Add drained vegetables and tofu. Cover and refrigerate for several hours.

3. Just before serving, combine nonfat sour cream, lemon juice, and garlic. Stir in rice and mix well. Arrange mixture into a ring on a large serving platter.

4. Place marinated vegetables and tofu in center of ring and serve with pita chips or crackers.

Makes 6 servings of 12 appetizers
(not including crackers)

Each serving contains:
142 calories, 6 gm. protein, 29 gm. carbohydrate, 1 gm. fat,
28 mg. sodium, 2 mg. cholesterol, 3 gm. fiber

ADA Exchange Value
2 Vegetable, 1 Bread
6% of total calories are from fat

◆ Tomato Cucumber Salad ◆

1/2 English cucumber cut in small cubes
4 small plum tomatoes cubed
3 T. seasoned rice-wine vinegar
4 leaves Bibb lettuce

1. Mix cucumber, tomato and vinegar together.
2. Place lettuce leaves on plate and divide the cucumber mixture on each.

Makes 4 servings.

Each serving contains:
26 calories, 1 gm. protein, 6 gm. carbohydrate, <1 gm. fat,
10 mg. sodium, 0 cholesterol, 2 gm. fiber

ADA Exchange Value
1 Vegetable
0 calories are from fat

◆ Brown Rice Salad ◆

2 cups cooked brown rice
2 T. green onion tops, chopped
2 T. red bell pepper, chopped
2 T. corn, cooked and drained
2 T. peas, cooked
1/4 cup orange juice
1 T. peanut butter
1 T. low-sodium soy sauce

1. Combine rice, onion, red pepper, corn, and peas in a serving bowl.
2. In a small bowl, mix together orange juice, peanut butter, and soy sauce.
3. Pour dressing over rice and vegetables. Chill.

Makes 2 1/2 cups, or 5 servings.

Each serving contains:
113 calories, 3 gm. protein, 21 gm. carbohydrate, 2 gm. fat,
234 mg. sodium, 0 cholesterol, 2 gm. fiber

ADA Exchange Value
1 Vegetable, 1 Bread
19% of total calories are from fat

◆ California Citrus Salad ◆

2 oranges, peeled and sliced into 12 rounds
1 medium-sized red onion, peeled and
    sliced
Lettuce leaves
1/2 cup Herbed Citrus Dressing (pg. 82)

1. Line 4 salad plates with lettuce leaves.
2. Place 3 orange slices decoratively on each plate,
followed by onion slices or rings.
3. Spoon 2 T. Herbed Citrus Dressing on each salad
and serve.

Makes 4 servings.

Each serving contains:
41 calories, 1 gm. protein, 10 gm. carbohydrate, <1 gm. fat,
negligible sodium, 0 cholesterol, 2 gm. fiber

ADA Exchange Value
1/2 Fruit, 1/2 Vegetable
4% of total calories are from fat

◆ Caesar Salad ◆

This is a different and fun way to serve the traditional
Caesar Salad. You pick it up with your hands and eat it
leaf by leaf.

1 head Romaine lettuce
1 clove garlic, minced
1 T. extra virgin olive oil
1/2 tsp. dry mustard
1/2 tsp. fresh ground pepper
1/4 tsp. Worcestershire sauce
3 T. white wine vinegar
1 T. fresh lemon juice
2 T. water
2 egg whites
1/2 cup Crunchy Croutons (pg. 178)
2 T. freshly grated Parmesan cheese

1. Cut bottom off romaine and remove leaves.
Trim, wash, and pat dry.

2. Put garlic, olive oil, mustard, pepper,
Worcestershire sauce, vinegar, lemon juice, water, and
egg whites in food processor. Using steel blade, turn
until well blended.

3. Arrange romaine leaves on one large plate (or 4
small ones). Pour dressing over bottom half of leaves.
Put croutons and Parmesan cheese on top.

◆ ◆ ◆

Makes 4 servings.

Beyond Alfalfa Sprouts & Cheese

Each serving contains:
74 calories, 4 gm. protein, 4 gm. carbohydrate, 4 gm. fat,
109 mg. sodium, 2 mg. cholesterol, 1 gm. fiber

ADA Exchange Value
1 Vegetable, 1 Fat
50% of total calories are from fat

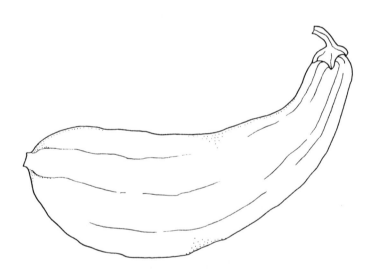

◆ Cucumber and Onions in Yogurt ◆

1 medium cucumber, washed and sliced
1 small red onion, peeled and sliced
1/2 cup Yogurt Cheese (pg. 177)
1 T. lemon juice
1 tsp. Dijon-style mustard
1 tsp. fresh parsley, minced
1 tsp. fresh thyme, minced,
    or 1/2 tsp. dried
Fresh ground black pepper

1. Put sliced cucumbers and onion into a glass or ceramic bowl.
2. Combine remaining ingredients and mix well.
3. Pour dressing over vegetables, mix well, and allow to marinate for several hours. Serve.

Makes 2 cups. 1 serving = 1/2 cup

Each serving contains:

33 calories, 2 gm. protein, 5 gm. carbohydrate, <1 gm. fat,
22 mg. sodium, 2 mg. cholesterol, 1 gm. fiber

ADA Exchange Value
1 Vegetable
<5% of total calories are from fat

◆ Shredded Vegetable Salad ◆

1 lb. cabbage, shredded (about 4 cups)
1 small jicama, peeled and cut in julienne
    strips (about 2" long)
    (or substitute a small cucumber)
1 medium carrot, scrubbed and shredded
3 green onions, chopped
1/4 cup balsamic vinegar
1 T. olive oil
1 tsp. ginger, freshly grated
2 T. fresh orange juice

1. Combine cabbage, jicama, carrot, and green
onion. Place in a large bowl.
2. Combine remaining ingredients as a dressing
and pour over vegetables. Cover and refrigerate until
well chilled.

Makes about 7 cups. 1 serving = 1 cup.

Each serving contains:
50 calories, 1 gm. protein, 7 gm. carbohydrate, 2 gm. fat,
17 mg. sodium, 0 cholesterol, 3 gm. fiber

ADA Exchange Value
2 Vegetable
36% of total calories are from fat

◆ Waldorf Salad ◆

2 medium apples, cored and chopped
(toss in lemon water to keep from
turning brown)
2 stalks celery, chopped
1/2 cup raisins
1/4 cup chopped walnuts
1/2 cup fat-free sour cream
2 T. low-fat mayonnaise
1/8 tsp. nutmeg

Mix all ingredients together well. Cover and chill.

Makes 4 servings.

Each serving contains:
123 calories, 3 gm. protein, 20 gm. carbohydrate, 6 gm. fat,
49 mg. sodium, 5 mg. cholesterol, 3 gm. fiber

ADA Exchange Value
1 Vegetable, 1 Fruit, 1 Fat
44% of total calories are from fat

◆ Mandarin Orange Mold ◆

2 10 1/2-oz. cans mandarin oranges in
  own juice (no sugar added)
2 T. Agar (found in health food stores)
2 cups nonfat cottage cheese
2 T. fructose
1/3 cup walnuts

1. Drain liquid from oranges into small sauce pan.
Add Agar and mix. Heat to a simmer and cook until
Agar is dissolved.

2. Put cottage cheese into food processor and whip
until smooth.

3. Add liquid and blend.

4. Add fructose and walnuts, and quickly blend
into mixture.

5. Pour into 1-quart mold and chill.

Makes 8 servings.

Each serving contains:
129 calories, 8 gm. protein, 19 gm. carbohydrate, 3 gm. fat,
14 mg. sodium, 3 mg. cholesterol, 1 gm. fiber

ADA Exchange Value
1 Fruit, 1 Low-fat Meat
21% of total calories are from fat

◆ Chilled Couscous Vegetable Salad ◆

8 oz. couscous (about 1 1/2 cups)
1 cup Vegetable Stock (*pg. 54)
1 T. fresh thyme chopped or 1/2 tsp. dried
2 T. wine vinegar
1 cup frozen baby peas (thaw by running
    cold water over them in colander)
1 cup frozen corn kernels (thaw as for
    baby peas)
2 large tomatoes, peeled, seeded, and
    chopped
2 scallions, sliced thin
1 T. fresh basil, chopped, or 1/2 tsp. dried
6 romaine leaves, washed and dried

1. Place couscous in a large bowl. Pour 1 cup boiling water over couscous and let stand.

2. In saucepan, bring Vegetable Stock to boil, add thyme and vinegar. Boil to reduce to 3/4 cups.

3. Add peas and corn to liquid and turn off heat.

4. Toss tomatoes, scallions, and basil into couscous.

5. Add liquid to couscous and mix well. Cover and refrigerate 2 hours before serving.

6. To serve, top a romaine leaf with couscous mixture.

◆ ◆ ◆

Makes 6 servings.

Each serving contains:
197 calories, 7 gm. protein, 44 gm. carbohydrate, 2 gm. fat,
34 mg. sodium, 0 cholesterol, 6 gm. fiber

ADA Exchange Value
3 Bread
9% of total calories are from fat

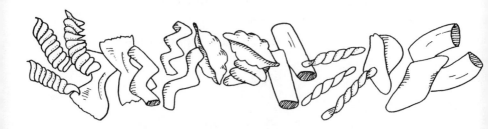

◆ Macaroni Bean Salad ◆

1 lb. macaroni
6 cups cooked beans
2 cups nonfat cottage cheese
1/2 cup low-fat mayonnaise
1/2 cup low-fat sour cream
1 tsp. dill seasoning
4 cups sliced celery
1 cup grated carrots
16 oz. frozen baby peas (rinsed in cold
   water to thaw)

1. Cook macaroni until tender. Rinse with cold water.
2. In large bowl, mix macaroni and beans together.
3. In food processor, using steel blade, process cottage cheese until very creamy; add mayonnaise, sour cream, and seasonings. Purée.
4. Pour mixture over macaroni and beans. Mix together well, cover, and refrigerate for at least 2 hours.

Makes 12 servings.

Each serving contains:
311 calories, 17 gm. protein, 50 gm. carbohydrate, 5 gm. fat,
124 mg. sodium, 5 mg. cholesterol, 3 gm. fiber

ADA Exchange Value
1 Vegetable, 3 Bread, 1 Lean Meat
15% of total calories are from fat

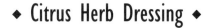

◆ Citrus Herb Dressing ◆

1/2 medium-sized red bell pepper, cut up
2 medium tomatoes, cut up
1/2 cup loosely packed fresh basil leaves
2 cloves garlic, peeled
1/2 cup fresh orange juice
1/2 cup loosely packed fresh parsley
1/4 cup raspberry vinegar
1 T. dry mustard
2 tsp. fresh thyme leaves, or 1 tsp. dried
2 tsp. fresh tarragon, or 1 tsp. dried
2 tsp. fresh oregano, or 1 tsp. dried
Ground black pepper

Combine all ingredients in a blender or food processor and blend until puréed.

Makes approximately 1 1/2 cups. 1 serving = 2 T.

Each serving contains:
13 calories, <1 gm. protein, 3 gm. carbohydrate, 0 fat,
2 mg. sodium, 0 cholesterol, <1 gm. fiber

ADA Exchange Value
1/2 Vegetable
0 calories are from fat

•••

Delicious Main Dishes

•••

◆ Stuffed Peppers with Rice and Tofu ◆

6 green or red bell peppers
Water

Filling:

20 oz. firm or regular tofu, crumbled
1/2 cup onion, minced
1/2 cup celery, minced
2 egg whites
1/2 cup 1% milk
1 cup cooked brown rice
4 cups Basic Tomato Sauce (pg. 169)

1. Preheat oven to 350 degrees.
2. Core each pepper, rinse, and steam or parboil about 5 minutes. Drain and cool.
3. Combine tofu and remaining filling ingredients. Stuff peppers with mixture and place in a square baking dish.
4. Pour Basic Tomato Sauce evenly over peppers and bake 45 to 50 minutes.

◆ ◆ ◆

Makes 6 servings.

Each serving contains:

175 calories, 11 gm. protein, 22 gm. carbohydrate, 6 gm. fat, 291 mg. sodium, <1 mg. cholesterol, 4 gm. fiber

ADA Exchange Value

1/2 Bread, 1 Lean Meat, 2 Vegetable
31% of total calories are from fat

◆ Chili ◆

1 pound cooked beans (about 6 cups)
2 medium onions, chopped
1 clove garlic, minced
2 green bell peppers, chopped
1 T. chili powder
1/2 tsp. cayenne
1 28-oz. can diced tomatoes with juice
1 28-oz. can tomato sauce
16 oz. frozen corn (rinsed in cold water
   to thaw)
1 pound macaroni

1. Put beans in crockpot or Dutch oven.

2. Saute onions and garlic in a skillet sprayed with a nonstick spray until soft.

3. Add green peppers, cover, cook on low heat 3 minutes. Uncover, add chili powder and red pepper, and cook on medium high heat for 2 minutes, stirring constantly.

4. Put mixture in with beans. Add tomatoes and tomato sauce.

5. Cook all day in croc pot, or on low heat for 2 hours on the stove.

6. Add corn to chili.

7. Cook macaroni and mix in the chili.

Makes 10 servings.

Delicious Main Dishes

Each serving contains:
274 calories, 12 gm. protein, 56 gm. carbohydrate, 2 gm. fat,
493 mg. sodium, 0 cholesterol, 14 gm. fiber

ADA Exchange Value
3 Bread, 2 Vegetable
6% of total calories are from fat

◆ Mexican Peppers ◆

4 green bell peppers
1 medium onion, chopped
1 clove garlic, minced
1 T. chili powder
1/2 tsp. cumin
1/4 tsp. ground red pepper
1 14-oz. can diced tomatoes with juice
1/2 cup corn meal
1 cup black beans
1 cup corn kernels
6 oz. nonfat cheddar cheese

1. Cut the tops off green peppers, remove seeds. Blanch in boiling water for 5 minutes. Drain on paper towels, upside down.

2. Sauté onion and garlic in a large skillet until soft.

3. Add chili powder, cumin, red pepper, tomatoes, and corn meal. Mix well, cover and simmer on low heat for 10 minutes.

4. Add beans, corn, and cheese to mixture. Mix well.

5. Place peppers in baking dish and fill each with the bean mixture. Place baking pan in another pan with 1/2 inch water. Cover lightly with foil and bake at 350 degrees for 35 minutes.

◆ ◆ ◆

Makes 4 servings.

Delicious Main Dishes

Each serving contains:
240 calories, 18 gm. protein, 41 gm. carbohydrate, 2 gm. fat,
359 mg. sodium, 2 mg. cholesterol, 10 gm.

ADA Exchange Value
2 Bread, 1 Lean Meat, 2 Vegetable
8% of total calories are from fat

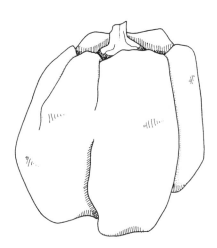

◆ Moussaka ◆

2 medium eggplants, peeled and sliced
    into 1/4 inch rounds
1 medium onion, chopped
1 clove garlic, minced
2 cups zucchini, grated
1 27 1/2-oz. can diced tomatoes
    in juice
2 T. tomato paste
1/8 tsp. allspice
1/8 tsp. nutmeg
2 cups nonfat ricotta cheese
1/2 cup Parmesan cheese, shredded

Fat-Free White Sauce

1 1/2 cups nonfat milk
1 tsp. Butter Buds
3 T. Cream of Rice
1/4 tsp. ground white pepper

    1. Steam eggplant 5 minutes and set on paper towels.

    2. In large skillet, sprayed with nonstick spray, sauté onion and garlic until soft. Add zucchini and cook until tender.

    3. Add tomatoes, tomato paste, allspice, and nutmeg. Simmer for 15 minutes, uncovered.

4. Spray 8" x 13" baking dish with nonstick spray. Layer half the eggplant in the dish.
5. Spread vegetable mixture over the eggplant. Layer remaining eggplant over the top.
6. Mix ricotta cheese and Parmesan cheese together and spread over eggplant.
7. Heat milk in sauce pan until boiling. Slowly add Cream of Rice, Butter Buds, and pepper. Simmer until thick.
8. Pour white sauce over the top of eggplant.
9. Bake in a 350-degree oven for 45 minutes. Let stand 10 minutes before serving.

Makes 6 serving.

Each serving contains:
133 calories, 13 gm. protein, 18 gm. carbohydrate, 2 gm. fat,
242 mg. sodium, 6 mg. cholesterol, 4 gm. fiber

ADA Exchange Value
1 Lean Meat, 3 Vegetable
14% of total calories are from fat

◆ Eggplant Casserole ◆

3 pounds eggplant, peeled and sliced
1 medium onion, sliced
2 pounds mushrooms, cleaned and
    quartered
2 green bell peppers, sliced
1 tsp. Italian seasonings
1 27-oz. can diced tomatoes
1 27-oz. can tomato sauce
3 3/4 cups nonfat milk
3/4 cup Cream of Rice cereal, dry
4 oz. feta cheese

1. Spray a cookie sheet with nonstick spray. Place eggplant on sheet. Spray eggplant lightly with nonstick spray. Bake at 350 degrees for 15 minutes.

2. Spray a Dutch oven with nonstick spray and sauté onions and green pepper until soft.

3. Add seasoning to onions and peppers and mix well.. Add diced tomatoes and tomato sauce. Simmer for 30 minutes.

4. Put mushrooms in sauté pan, cover, and simmer 5 minutes. Uncover and saute until liquid is absorbed.

5. Heat milk to boiling. Slowly add Cream of Rice, stirring constantly until thickened. Turn off heat and mix in feta cheese.

6. In a large baking dish, put a layer of eggplant. Cover with half the sauce. Spread mushrooms evenly

over eggplant. Pour Cream of Rice mixture over mushrooms and pour remaining sauce over top.

7. Bake uncovered 45 minutes at 350 degrees. Let stand 15 minutes before serving.

Makes 6 servings.

Note: This recipe is higher in sodium than most of our recipes. You may choose to use low-sodium canned tomatoes.

Each serving contains:
282 calories, 16 gm. protein, 47 gm. carbohydrate, 6 gm. fat,
1446 mg. sodium, 19 mg. cholesterol, 13 gm. fiber

ADA Exchange Value
1 Bread, 1 Medium Fat Meat, 2 Vegetable,
1/2 Nonfat milk
19% of total calories are from fat

◆ Tofu Stroganoff ◆

20 oz. firm tofu, drained, pressed, and
   cut into 1/2-inch slices about 2-inches
   long
2 T. low-sodium soy sauce
1/2 cup green onions, chopped
1 lb. mushrooms, thinly sliced
1 T. flour
1/2 cup white wine
1 cup nonfat sour cream
1 T. tomato purée
2 T. parsley

1. Spray a large skillet with nonstick spray and heat
to medium. Add tofu and low-sodium soy sauce. Sauté
tofu and turn carefully until lightly browned. Remove
from pan.
   2. Add onions and mushrooms to pan and sauté 3
to 4 minutes. Sprinkle flour over mixture. Add wine,
sour cream, and tomato purée. Stir until well blended
and slightly thickened.
   3. Gently stir in tofu, cover, and simmer 2 to 3
minutes Serve over brown rice or noodles. Sprinkle
parsley on top.

◆ ◆ ◆

Makes 4 large servings.

Delicious Main Dishes

Each serving contains:
147 calories, 15 gm. protein, 15 gm. carbohydrate, 3 gm. fat,
162 mg. sodium, 5 mg. cholesterol, 5 gm. fiber

ADA Exchange Value
2 Lean Meat, 1 Vegetable, 1/2 Fat
18% of total calories are from fat

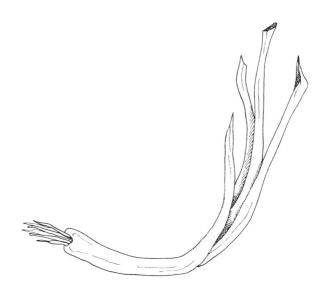

◆ Spinach and Artichoke Pie ◆ with Rice Crust

1 package frozen artichoke hearts
  (8 to 9 oz.)
1/4 cup onions, chopped fine
1 cup spinach, cooked and drained
1/2 cup nonfat cottage cheese
1/4 cup nonfat sour cream
Ground pepper
2 T. Parmesan cheese, grated
Rice Crust (pg 174)

1. Preheat oven to 350 degrees.

2. Prepare artichokes according to package directions. Drain and set aside.

3. Sauté onions in a skillet sprayed with nonstick spray.

4. Layer drained artichoke hearts on top of Rice Crust.

5. Combine spinach, cottage cheese, sour cream, cooked onions, and ground pepper in a food processor, pulsing just to blend or mix. Pour mixture into Rice Crust lined with artichokes. Sprinkle with Parmesan cheese and bake for 20 minutes or until just heated through.

Makes 8 servings.

Delicious Main Dishes

Each serving contains:
100 calories, 7 gm. protein, 17 gm. carbohydrate, 1 gm. fat,
112 mg. sodium, 2 mg. cholesterol, 3 gm. fiber

ADA Exchange Value
1 Bread, 1 Vegetable
9% of total calories are from fat

◆ Lasagna ◆

1 pound lasagna noodles, undercooked
2 tsp. olive oil
2 medium onions, sliced
2 tsp. Italian herbs
1 pound sliced mushrooms
2 28-oz. cans diced tomatoes
2 cups nonfat cottage cheese
2 cups low-fat ricotta cheese
1 10-oz. package frozen chopped spinach,
   thawed with water squeezed out
1 tsp. Italian herbs
1/2 tsp. garlic powder
1/4 cup grated Parmesan cheese

1. Heat olive oil in skillet; add onions, cook until soft. Add 2 tsp. herbs, mix and remove from pan. Set aside.

2. Put mushrooms in skillet, cover and simmer for 5 minutes. Remove cover and sauté until liquid is absorbed.

3. Add onions to mushrooms. Add diced tomatoes and simmer 30 minutes uncovered.

4. In food processor, place cottage cheese and whip until smooth. Add ricotta cheese and whip together. Add spinach, 1 tsp. herbs, garlic powder, Parmesan cheese and pulse until well blended.

5. In a baking dish, layer noodles, cheese mixture, noodles, half the sauce, noodles, and remaining sauce.

6. Bake at 350 degrees for 1 hour. Let stand 15 minutes before serving.

(Note: This is even better if you make it the day ahead and reheat it for 30 minutes in a 325-degree oven before serving.)

◆ ◆ ◆

Makes 8 servings.

Each serving contains:
240 calories, 21 gm. protein, 33 gm. carbohydrate, 4 gm. fat, 510 mg. sodium, 10 mg. cholesterol, 6 gm. fiber

ADA Exchange Value
2 Bread, 2 Lean Meat, 1 Vegetable
15% of total calories are from fat

◆ Tamale Pie ◆

1 cup corn meal
1 cup unbleached flour
1 T. baking powder
1 T. fructose
1 cup cooked corn kernels
1 cup low-fat buttermilk
2 egg whites

Topping

2 cups cooked pinto beans
1 cup green chili salsa
1 cup hoop cheese

1. Combine corn meal, flour, baking powder, fructose, and corn in a large bowl.
2. Mix buttermilk and egg whites together. Pour into dry ingredients and mix together.
3. Pour into a 9-inch baking pan that has been sprayed with nonstick spray.
4. Spread beans, salsa, and cheese evenly over the top.
5. Bake in a 350-degree oven for 35 minutes.

Makes 6 servings.

Delicious Main Dishes

Each serving contains:
278 calories, 16 gm. protein
53 gm. carbohydrate, 2 gm. fat, 180 mg. sodium,
3 mg. cholesterol, 13 gm. fiber

ADA Exchange Value
3 Bread, 1 Lean Meat
6% of total calories are from fat

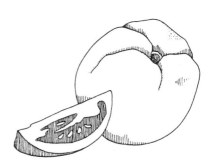

◆ Lentil Loaf ◆

1 1/2 cups lentils
4 cups water
1 14 1/2-oz. can diced tomatoes
    with juice
2 bay leaves
1 cup low-fat cheddar cheese
1 cup mozzarella cheese
8 oz. diced mushrooms
1 cup cooked brown rice
1 T. fresh chopped parsley
2 tsp. dried herb blend
1 T. fresh lemon juice
6 egg whites, beaten
1/2 tsp. fresh ground black pepper

1. Put the lentils, water, diced tomatoes, and bay leaves in a sauce pan. Cover and simmer until the lentils are tender, about 60 minutes. Remove from heat and remove bay leaves.

2. Preheat oven to 375 degrees.

3. Mix all ingredients into lentils and mix together well.

4. Spray a 2-pound loaf pan with a nonstick spray.

5. Spoon lentil mixture in pan and smooth top.

6. Bake uncovered for 1 1/2 hours, until all liquid is absorbed and mixture is brown on top.

◆ ◆ ◆

Makes 8 servings.

Each serving contains:
178 calories, 14 gm. protein, 15 gm. carbohydrate, 7 gm. fat,
326 mg. sodium, 23 mg. cholesterol, 3 gm. fiber

ADA Exchange Value
1 Bread, 1 Lean Meat, 1 Fat
38% of total calories are from fat

◆ Pastitsio ◆

This is a Greek dish that is normally made with ground
beef. However, it works deliciously with beans.

> 2 cups cooked beans (black, navy,
>   kidney, or mixed)
> 1 small onion, chopped
> 1 27-oz. can diced tomatoes with juice
> 3 T. fresh chopped parsley
> 1/4 tsp. cinnamon
> 1/2 tsp. ground black pepper
> 1 lb. ziti
> 4 egg whites
> 1/2 cup Parmesan cheese
> Greek White Sauce

1. Preheat oven to 350 degrees.

2. In skillet sprayed with nonstick spray, sauté
onion until soft.

3. Add beans, tomatoes, parsley, cinnamon, and
pepper. Mix and simmer 15 minutes, uncovered.

4. Cook ziti in boiling water, until slightly underdone. Drain well.

5. Whip egg whites until soft peaks form. Mix
into ziti. Mix in Parmesan cheese.

6. Put ziti in large, deep baking dish. Top with
bean mixture, then with Greek White Sauce. Bake for
30 minutes. Let stand 10 to 15 minutes before serving.

Greek White Sauce

3 cups nonfat milk
2 tsp. Butter Buds
1/2 tsp. ground white pepper
3/4 cup dry Cream of Rice cereal
1/4 cup Parmesan cheese

Heat milk to simmer. Slowly add remaining ingredients. Simmer until sauce is thickened.

Makes 8 servings.

Each serving contains:
312 calories, 17 gm. protein, 53 gm. carbohydrate, 4 gm. fat, 433 mg. sodium, 8 mg. cholesterol, 7 gm. fiber

ADA Exchange Value
3 Bread, 1 Lean Meat, 2 Vegetable
10% of total calories are from fat

◆ Stir "Fried" Tofu and Vegetables ◆

Marinade

1/2 lb. tofu, diced
1/4 cup low-sodium soy sauce
1/4 cup water
1 clove garlic, crushed
2 tsp. fresh ginger, minced
1/4 tsp. cinnamon
1/4 tsp. ground allspice
1/8 tsp. ground cloves

Sauce

1/2 cup strained marinade
1/2 cup Vegetable Stock (pg. 54)
1 T. sherry (optional)
1 tsp. fructose
1 tsp. vinegar
1 T. cornstarch

Vegetables

1 clove garlic, minced
2 tsp. fresh ginger, minced
1 small onion, sliced
1 cup fresh mushrooms, washed and sliced
1 stalk celery, sliced

1 T. almonds, slivered
1/2 lb. Chinese pea pods, fresh or frozen
1/2 lb. bean sprouts

1. Combine tofu and rest of ingredients for marinade in saucepan. Simmer for 10 minutes. Drain and reserve 1/2 cup marinade.
2. Combine all ingredients for sauce in a bowl.
3. Spray a wok or large frying pan with nonstick spray. Heat to high heat, stir in garlic, ginger, onion, and stir fry for 2 to 3 minutes. Remove to bowl.
4. Repeat same process as in step 3 with mushrooms, tofu, celery, almonds, and snow peas. Stir fry just until peas are bright green.
5. Return other ingredients to wok. Add bean sprouts. Stir, then pour in sauce. Cook and stir carefully until sauce glazes vegetables. Serve over rice, noodles or other grains.

Makes 6 generous servings.

Each serving contains:
121 calories, 9 gm. protein, 16 gm. carbohydrate, 3 gm. fat,
583 mg. sodium, 0 cholesterol, 4 gm. fiber

ADA Exchange Value
1 Lean Meat, 3 Vegetable

25% of total calories are from fat

◆ Mushroom Lasagna ◆

1 pound lasagna noodles, undercooked
1 onion, chopped
1 1/2 pounds sliced mushrooms
15 oz. nonfat ricotta cheese
2 cups nonfat cottage cheese
1 tsp. Italian seasoning
1/4 cup Parmesan cheese, grated

Sauce

3 cups nonfat milk
3 T. cornstarch
1/2 tsp. white pepper
1/2 cup Parmesan cheese, grated

1. In skillet sprayed with nonstick spray, sauté onion until soft. Add mushrooms; cover and cook on low heat for 5 minutes. Uncover and sauté until all liquid is absorbed.

2. In food processor, using steel blade, whip ricotta, cottage cheese, Italian seasoning, and 1/4 cup Parmesan.

3. In a baking dish, layer 1/2 of the noodles; spread cheese mixture over them and evenly spread mushroom mixture on top of cheese.

4. Layer remaining noodles over top.

5. Mix milk, cornstarch, and pepper in sauce pan. Bring to a slow boil and stir until thick. Add Parmesan cheese and mix well.

6. Pour sauce over lasagna.

7. Bake in preheated 350-degree oven for 35 minutes. Let stand 10 minutes before serving.

◆ ◆ ◆

Makes 8 servings.

Each serving contains:
294 calories, 24 gm. protein, 30 gm. carbohydrate, 9 gm. fat, 274 mg. sodium, 47 mg. cholesterol, 3 gm. fiber

ADA Exchange Value
1 1/2 Bread, 3 Lean Meat, 1 Vegetable
28% of total calories are from fat

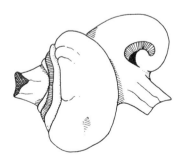

◆ Zucchini Casserole ◆

3 to 4 medium-sized zucchini, washed
   and sliced thin
1 large onion, chopped
1 14 1/2-oz. can tomatoes
1 T. fresh basil, minced, or 1 1/2 tsp. dried
2 tsp. fresh rosemary leaves, or 1 tsp. dried
1 1/2 cups brown rice, cooked
1/4 cup Mozzarella cheese, shredded

1. Spray a large skillet with nonstick spray. Heat to medium heat, then sauté onions until soft and beginning to brown.

2. Add zucchini and sauté until lightly cooked. Add tomatoes, basil, rosemary, and rice. Cover, reduce heat, and simmer 15 to 20 minutes.

3. Remove lid. Add cheese. Recover and allow cheese to melt. Serve.

◆ ◆ ◆

Makes four 1-cup servings.

Each serving contains:
167 calories, 7 gm. protein, 32 gm. carbohydrate,
3 gm. fat, 232 mg. sodium, 4 mg. cholesterol, 5 gm. fiber

ADA Exchange Value
1 1/2 Bread, 1 Lean Meat, 1/2 Fat
16% of total calories are from fat

◆ Guiltless Pizza ◆

1 lb. frozen bread dough, thawed
1/2 cup Basic Tomato Sauce (pg. 169)
1 cup part-skim mozzarella cheese,
    shredded (about 2 oz.)
1 firm tomato, sliced
1 small onion, sliced
1/4 lb. mushrooms, sliced
2 T. Parmesan cheese

1. Preheat oven to 450 degrees.
2. Spread bread dough out on an 8-inch pizza pan or on a cookie sheet.
3. Pour on Tomato Sauce and spread evenly over crust. Add vegetables and finish with Parmesan cheese.
4. Bake for 15 to 20 minutes or until crust is browned. Slice and serve.

Makes 8 servings.

Each serving contains:
184 calories, 8 gm. protein, 30 gm. carbohydrate, 4 gm. fat,
386 mg. sodium, 5 mg. cholesterol, 1 gm. fiber

ADA Exchange Value
1 1/2 Bread, 1 Lean Meat, 1 Vegetable
18% of total calories are from fat

···

Beans, Rice, Potatoes & Pasta

···

◆ About Beans ◆

Dried, cooked beans are another staple of vegetarian-style cooking. Pinto beans, kidney beans, or black beans are generally used. Beans are high in complex carbohydrates and are an excellent source of protein, fiber, and trace minerals. Beans are often considered to be high in calories, but the high calories are usually the result of added ingredients such as fat. Without added fat, beans are healthy and nutritious and very inexpensive. We recommend cooking beans ahead and storing them in the freezer in one or two cup containers. Canned beans can be used but will usually be much higher in salt content and often have a different texture. Dried beans are very inexpensive and are available all year around. Look for them in the rice and pasta section of your grocery store.

◆ Basic Beans ◆

    1 lb. dried beans such as pinto, kidney,
        garbanzo, or black beans
    Water or broth to cover
    1 onion
    2 or 3 stalks celery
    1 clove garlic

1. Place beans in a strainer or sieve and rinse under running water.

2. Place beans in a large bowl and cover with water.

3. Let beans soak for 6 to 8 hours or overnight.

4. Drain beans and place in a large pot.

5. Cover with fresh water or broth.

6. Chop onion and 2 to 3 stalks of celery into large chunks. Peel garlic and cut in half. Add to pot of beans.

7. Bring beans to a boil. Reduce to simmer and cook until done. Time will vary according to type of bean.

8. Cool slightly and divide beans and liquid into freezer containers.

9. Store in freezer until needed. Use within 3 to 4 months.

Makes 10 servings.

Each serving contains:
158 calories, 9 gm. protein, 30 gm. carbohydrate, 1 gm. fat, 13 mg. sodium, 0 cholesterol, 12 gm. fiber

ADA Exchange Value
2 Bread, 1/2 Lean Meat
4 % of total calories are from fat

◆ Guiltless Refried Beans ◆

2 cups cooked pinto beans, including
bean juice
1/2 tsp. chili powder

1. Spray a heavy skillet with nonstick spray and heat.
2. Add beans and juice, mashing and stirring beans until desired consistency.
3. Add chili powder and stir to mix.

Makes 6 servings.

Each serving contains:
80 calories, 5 gm. protein, 15 gm. carbohydrate,
negligible fat, 7 mg. sodium, 0 cholesterol, 6 gm. fiber

ADA Exchange Value
1 Bread
Negligible fat calories

◆ Mexican Rice ◆

2 tomatoes, chopped into large chunks
1/2 onion, chopped into large chunks
2 cloves garlic, peeled and cut in half
1 cup brown rice, uncooked
1 T. corn oil
1/4 tsp. chili powder
1 small bunch cilantro
1 1/2 cups vegetable broth or water

1. Combine tomatoes, onion and garlic in a blender and purée.
2. Strain mixture into a small bowl and add chili powder.
3. Heat oil in a heavy pan or skillet.
4. Brown the rice in hot oil, stirring constantly so it will not burn.
5. When rice is browned, add tomato mixture and broth or water.
6. Place bunch of cilantro on top of rice—do not stir in.
7. Bring to a boil, then reduce heat to simmer.
8. Cover and cook approximately 45 minutes or until rice is done and all liquid is absorbed.
9. Carefully remove cilantro. Stir slightly and serve.

Makes 5 servings. 1 serving = 1/3 cup

Each serving contains:
87 calories, 2 gm. protein, 13 gm. carbohydrate, 4 gm. fat,
418 mg. sodium, negligible cholesterol, 2 gm. fiber

ADA Exchange Value
1 Bread, 1/2 Fat
14 % of total calories are from fat

◆ Skillet Cornbread ◆

This is a modified version of a classic recipe from the South. It will turn out best when you use a 6-inch cast iron skillet.

> 1 cup yellow corn meal
> 3/4 tsp. baking soda
> 1 cup buttermilk
> 1 T. vegetable oil

1. Preheat oven to 400 degrees.
2. Combine corn meal, baking soda, and buttermilk.
3. Heat oil over medium high heat until very hot. Lightly tip skillet to oil sides as well as bottom.
4. Pour cornmeal batter into hot skillet. Place in oven and bake for 25 minutes.
5. Remove from oven. Loosen sides and bottom then turn out upside down on a bread board or serving platter.

Makes 6 servings.

Each serving contains:
119 calories, 3 gm. protein, 20 gm. carbohydrate, 3 gm. fat, 187 mg. sodium, 2 mg. cholesterol, 1 gm. fiber

ADA Exchange Value
1 Bread, 1/2 Fat
23 % of total calories are from fat

◆ Pot Roasted Pasta ◆

1 T. olive oil
1 medium onion, sliced
3 carrots, cut in small matchstick strips
4 stalks celery, sliced
1 1/2 lb. mushrooms, washed and sliced
2 4-oz. cans sliced ripe olives (optional)
4 cups Basic Tomato Sauce (pg. 169)
1 28-oz. can diced tomatoes in juice
1 lb. pasta

1. Heat olive oil in a large Dutch oven. Sauté onions until soft. Add carrots, celery and cooked mushrooms to onions and mix well.

2. Add olives, Basic Tomato Sauce and canned tomatoes. Mix well. Bring to a simmer. Cook uncovered for 1 hour.

3. Cook pasta until just underdone. Drain well.

4. Mix pasta and sauce together and put into baking dish. Bake at 350 degrees for 30 minutes, covered.

Makes 8 servings.

Each serving contains:
267 calories, 9 gm. protein, 48 gm. carbohydrate, 6 gm. fat,
365 mg. sodium, 0 cholesterol, 7 gm. fiber

ADA Exchange Value
2 Bread, 2 Vegetable, 1 Fat
19 % of total calories are from fat

◆ Beans and Rice ◆

1 lb. red or black beans, washed and
  soaked several hours
1 large onion, chopped
6 cloves garlic, minced
8 cups water
1 cup cooked brown rice
Freshly ground pepper

  1. Combine pre-soaked beans in a large pot or
crockpot with onion, garlic, and water.
  2. Cover and cook at a simmer for 6 to 7 hours.
  3. When beans are tender, add cooked brown rice
and a few grinds of black pepper.

This is a good basic recipe for combining beans and
rice. Consider serving it in bowls topped with "Greens"
(pg. 160) and with cornbread accompaniment.

Makes 8 cups. 1 serving = 1 cup

Each serving contains:
164 calories, 10 gm. protein, 31 gm. carbohydrate, 1 gm. fat,
75 mg. sodium, 0 cholesterol, 12 gm. fiber

ADA Exchange Value
2 Bread
5 % of total calories are from fat

◆ Linguini with Limas and Mustard ◆

6 ripe plum tomatoes, seeded and cut in
   strips
1 1/2 cups Vegetable Stock (pg. 54)
2 cups frozen baby lima beans
3 scallions, thinly sliced
3 T. grainy mustard
1 lb. linguini

1. Cook linguini in large pot of boiling water until al dente. Drain in colander.

2. While linguini is cooking, bring vegetable broth to a boil. Add lima beans, scallions, and mustard. Slow boil for 7 minutes; add tomato slices and turn off heat.

3. Toss linguini in the broth. Serve.

Makes 6 servings.

Each serving contains:
223 calories, 9 gm. protein, 46 gm. carbohydrate, 1 gm. fat,
46 mg. sodium, 0 cholesterol, 4 gm. fiber

ADA Exchange Value
3 Bread
4 % of total calories are from fat

◆ Wagon Wheels and Beans ◆

1 T. olive oil
1 medium onion, chopped
2 green bell peppers, chopped
2 cloves garlic, minced
2 28-oz. cans diced tomatoes with juice
1/2 tsp. red pepper, crushed
2 T. chopped fresh cilantro
2 cups cooked pinto beans, rinsed in
   cool water
Freshly ground black pepper
1 lb. wagon wheel pasta, cooked al dente

1. Heat olive oil in large skillet. Cook onions, peppers, and garlic until soft.

2. Add tomatoes, red pepper, cilantro, beans, and black pepper. Simmer 10 minutes.

3. Add pasta to sauce and mix in gently.

Makes 6 servings.

Each serving contains:
267 calories, 10 gm. protein, 52 gm. carbohydrate, 3 gm. fat,
223 mg. sodium, 0 cholesterol, 8 gm. fiber

ADA Exchange Value
3 Bread, 1/2 Fat, 1 Vegetable
10 % of total calories are from fat

◆ Kashi Stroganoff ◆

2 1/4 cups water
1 tsp. vegetable seasoning
1 cup Kashi
1 medium onion, sliced
1 medium red bell pepper, sliced
8 oz. mushrooms, sliced
4 medium zucchini, sliced in small strips
1 cup nonfat sour cream

1. Bring water to boil. Add vegetable seasoning. Slowly add Kashi. Reduce heat to simmer, cover, and cook 25 minutes (until all water is absorbed). Let stand 5 minutes.

2. In a skillet sprayed with nonstick spray, sauté onions and peppers until soft. Add mushrooms, cover and cook on low heat 5 minutes. Uncover and add zucchini. Cook on high until water is absorbed.

3. Mix Kashi into vegetables. Add sour cream and stir in well. Serve hot or cold.

◆ ◆ ◆

Makes 6 servings.

Each serving contains:
85 calories, 4 gm. protein, 17 gm. carbohydrate, 1 gm. fat,
25 mg. sodium, 3 mg. cholesterol, 4 gm. fiber

ADA Exchange Value
1 Bread
11 % of total calories are from fat

◆ Noodles with Mushroom Yogurt Sauce ◆

1 lb. medium wide noodles
1 tsp. olive oil
1 medium onion, sliced
1 lb. mushrooms, sliced
1/2 cup dry vermouth
1 cup nonfat sour cream
1 cup plain nonfat yogurt
1/4 to 1/2 tsp. cayenne pepper
2 T. poppy seeds

1. Cook noodles al dente, drain, and set aside.

2. Heat olive oil in a large skillet or Dutch oven. Add onion and sauté until tender. Remove onions to holding plate. Add mushrooms to pan. Cover for 3 minutes. Uncover and cook until all liquid is absorbed and mushrooms are brown. Add vermouth and continue to cook until most of the vermouth is absorbed.

3. Return onions to pan, add sour cream, yogurt, pepper, and poppy seeds to mushrooms and mix well.

4. Refresh noodles with hot water in colander. Add noodles to yogurt mixture and mix well.

Makes 6 servings.

Each serving contains:
239 calories, 11 gm. protein, 45 gm. carbohydrate, 1 gm. fat, 43 mg. sodium, 2 mg. cholesterol, 3 gm. fiber

ADA Exchange Value
2 Bread, 1 Vegetable, 1/2 Nonfat Milk
4 % of total calories are from fat

◆ Barley, Beans, and Rice ◆

1 medium onion, chopped
8 oz. bell peppers (red, green, or yellow)
    chopped
8 oz. sliced mushrooms
1 cup long grain white rice
1 cup barley
4 cups Vegetable Stock (pg. 54)
2 cups cooked black beans

1. Spray a skillet with nonstick spray and sauté onions and peppers. Set aside.

2. In same skillet, sauté mushrooms in 2 T. of Vegetable Stock until all the liquid has been absorbed.

3. In a rice cooker or saucepan, place the vegetables, rice, barley and broth. Cover and simmer until all liquid has been absorbed.

4. In a colander, rinse beans well. Place in a large bowl.

5. Mix the rice mixture into the beans.

Makes 6 servings.

Each serving contains:
263 calories, 10 gm. protein, 55 gm. carbohydrate, 1 gm. fat,
8 mg. sodium, 0 cholesterol, 8 gm. fiber

ADA Exchange Value
3 Bread, 1 Vegetable
3 % of total calories are from fat

◆ Curried Lentils and Rice ◆

2 cloves garlic, minced
1 small onion, chopped
2 T. fresh ginger, minced
1/2 tsp. turmeric
1/2 tsp. cumin seeds, crushed
1/4 tsp. ground allspice
2 tsp. curry powder
1 cup lentils, washed
3/4 cup brown rice, washed
3 cups water

1. Spray a large, heavy pan with nonstick cooking spray. Heat to medium heat and sauté garlic, onion, and ginger until golden. Add spices and sauté 2 to 3 minutes more.

2. Add lentils and rice. Stir and add water. Bring to a boil, reduce heat, cover, and simmer 35 to 45 minutes. If more water is needed, add a few tablespoons at a time and simmer 10 minutes more.

3. Remove from heat. Let stand 10 to 15 minutes.

◆ ◆ ◆

Makes 6 cups. 1 serving = 1 cup
Each serving contains:
73 calories, 4 gm. protein, 14 gm. carbohydrate, <1 gm. fat,
71 mg. sodium, 0 cholesterol, 2 gm. fiber

ADA Exchange Value
1 Bread
3 % of total calories are from fat

◆ Potato and Black Beans ◆

4 medium potatoes, sliced thin with
   skin on
1 onion, chopped
2 cups cooked black beans
1/2 cup medium salsa
2 cups nonfat milk
2 T. cornstarch
1/2 tsp. white pepper
3 oz. reduced fat cheese

1. In a skillet sprayed with nonstick spray, sauté
onion until soft.
   2. Add beans and salsa to onion, cover and simmer
for 10 minutes.
   3. In another pan, mix milk, cornstarch, and
pepper together. Slowly bring to a boil, stirring constantly until thick.
   4. Add cheese. Turn off heat and mix together
well.
   5. In a 2 1/2-quart casserole dish sprayed with
nonstick spray, layer two of the potatoes. Pour 1/2
cheese sauce over them. Add the bean mixture, spread
evenly. Layer the two remaining potatoes over beans
and top with remaining cheese sauce.
   6. Bake, covered, in a preheated oven at 350
degrees for one hour. Remove cover and bake 10 more
minutes. Let sit 15 minutes before serving.

Makes 6 servings.

Each serving contains:
233 calories, 13 gm. protein, 41 gm. carbohydrate, 3 gm. fat,
126 mg. sodium, 9 mg. cholesterol, 8 gm. fiber

ADA Exchange Value
3 Bread, 1 Lean Meat
12 % of total calories are from fat

◆ Barley Casserole ◆

3 cups Vegetable Stock (pg. 54)
1 onion, chopped
1 lb. mushrooms, cleaned and sliced
2 cloves garlic, minced
1 T. low-sodium soy sauce
2 T. dry white wine
1 tsp. fresh thyme
1 cup barley, washed and drained
Ground black pepper

1. Preheat oven to 350 degrees.
2. Bring Vegetable Stock to a boil in a saucepan.
3. Spray a heavy-lidded oven-proof casserole dish
with nonstick spray. Sauté onions until tender and add
mushrooms and garlic. Continue to sauée for 2 to 3
minutes.

4. Add low-sodium soy sauce, wine, thyme, and cook for 3 minutes.

5. Stir in barley, then pour in hot Vegetable Stock and bring to a second boil. Add a little ground pepper, cover, and place in preheated oven.

6. Bake 30 to 40 minutes, or until barley is tender.

Makes 5 cups. 1 serving = 1/2 cup

Each serving contains:
88 calories, 4 gm. protein, 18 gm. carbohydrate, <1 gm. fat, 107 mg. sodium, 0 cholesterol, 3 gm. fiber

ADA Exchange Value
1 Bread
4 % of total calories are from fat

◆ Grilled Eggplant and Asparagus ◆

1/2 lb. asparagus, trimmed
2 Japanese eggplants, trimmed and sliced
1 medium onion, chopped
2 cloves garlic, chopped
2 T. fresh basil, or 1 tsp. dried
1 14-oz. can tomatoes
Olive-oil flavor nonstick cooking spray

1. Arrange asparagus and eggplant on a cookie sheet or platter, and spray vegetables with olive-oil-flavored nonstick spray lightly on all sides.

2. Grill vegetables on an outdoor grill or a stove-top grill until tender, turning often.

3. Spray a large skillet with nonstick spray and heat to medium. Add onions, garlic and basil, and cook 3 to 4 minutes. Add tomatoes and stir just to heat.

4. Arrange grilled vegetables on a serving platter or individual plates. Spoon tomato-onion sauce over vegetables and serve.

Makes 4 generous servings.

Each serving contains:
51 calories, 2 gm. protein, 11 gm. carbohydrate, <1 gm. fat,
199 mg. sodium, 0 cholesterol, 3 gm. fiber

ADA Exchange Value
2 Vegetables
8 % of total calories are from fat

◆ Rice and Vegetables ◆

1 T. olive oil
1 medium onion, chopped
1 clove garlic, minced
3 cups cooked brown rice
2 medium zucchini, shredded (about
 2 cups)
2 medium tomatoes, chopped
1/4 cup Parmesan cheese, grated
1 T. rice vinegar
1 tsp. marjoram
1/4 tsp. black pepper
1/4 tsp. dry mustard

1. Heat olive oil in skillet. Sauté onions and garlic until soft.

2. In a large bowl, mix all the ingredients. Put in 2-quart baking dish and bake at 350 degrees for 25 minutes. This can also be served cold.

◆ ◆ ◆

Makes 6 servings.

Each serving contains:
159 calories, 5 gm. protein, 27 gm. carbohydrate, 4 gm. fat,
67 mg. sodium, 3 mg. cholesterol, 3 gm. fiber

ADA Exchange Value
1 Bread, 2 Vegetable, 1 Fat
23 % of total calories are from fat

◆ Oven Roasted Potatoes ◆

4 small potatoes, scrubbed and cut into
   quarters, lengthwise
Olive oil spray
Paprika

1. Preheat oven to 450 degrees.
2. Place potato pieces on a nonstick sheet or
baking sheet lined with foil.
3. Spray potatoes lightly with olive oil spray and
sprinkle with paprika.
4. Bake for 20 minutes or until tender and brown.

◆ ◆ ◆

Makes 4 servings.

Each serving contains:
58 calories, 1 gm. protein, 13 gm. carbohydrate, <1 gm. fat,
6 mg. sodium, 0 cholesterol, 1 gm. fiber

ADA Exchange Value
1 Bread
0 calories are from fat

◆ Potatoes, Peppers, and Asparagus ◆

This is a great side dish. Try it with an egg on the side for breakfast.

> 2 medium red potatoes, halved and sliced thin
> 1 medium onion, peeled, cut in half from top to bottom, then sliced in 1/4-inch slivers
> 1/2 lb. asparagus, steamed crisp tender
> 1/2 small red bell pepper, sliced
> 1/2 small yellow bell pepper, sliced
> Freshly ground black pepper

1. Spray a large skillet with nonstick spray. Heat to medium high, then lay potato slices on bottom of pan with onions on top. Cover. Reduce heat and cook for about 5 minutes.

2. Turn potatoes and onion. Add peppers. Cover and cook for 5 minutes more or until potatoes are done.

3. Add several grinds of black pepper. Stir well, then add cooked asparagus. Heat through gently.

Makes 4 servings.

Each serving contains:
75 calories, 2 gm. protein, 17 gm. carbohydrate, <1 gm. fat, 7 mg. sodium, 0 cholesterol, 2 gm. fiber

ADA Exchange Value
1/2 Bread, 1 Vegetable
<2 % of total calories are from fat

◆ Spaghetti with Fresh Basil and Pine Nuts ◆

1 lb. spaghetti cooked al dente
1 T. olive oil
2 cloves garlic, minced
1 1/2 cup shredded basil leaves
1 cup Vegetable Stock (pg. 54)
1/2 cup pine nuts, roasted in a small skillet
1/2 cup grated Romano cheese
Freshly ground pepper to taste

1. Heat olive oil in large skillet and cook garlic until soft. Toss in basil and toss around skillet for 30 seconds. Add Vegetable Stock and simmer 10 minutes.
2. Toss pasta in the broth mixture. Add cheese and pepper. Toss to cover.

Makes 8 servings.

Each serving contains:
255 calories, 10 gm. protein, 34 gm. carbohydrate, 9 gm. fat, 133 mg. sodium, 6 mg. cholesterol, 2 gm. fiber

ADA Exchange Value
2 Bread, 2 Fat
31% of total calories are from fat

◆ Vermicelli and Peas ◆

1 lb. vermicelli, cooked al dente
1 T olive oil
2 medium onions, sliced
2 leeks, trimmed, cleaned and thinly sliced
Freshly ground black pepper
1 cup Vegetable Stock (pg. 54)
1 cup dry white vermouth
1 lb. baby frozen peas, rinsed in cold
    water to thaw

1. Heat olive oil in large skillet. Sauté onions and leeks until tender.
2. Add Vegetable Stock, vermouth, and pepper. Cook uncovered 10 minutes.
3. Add peas and heat. Toss in vermicelli and serve.

Makes 8 servings.

Each serving contains:
278 calories, 9 gm. protein, 46 gm. carbohydrate, 4 gm. fat,
41 mg. sodium, 50 mg. cholesterol, 4 gm. fiber

ADA Exchange Value
3 Bread, 1 Fat
14 % of total calories are from fat

◆ Pasta with Carrot Sauce ◆

3 cups Vegetable Stock (pg. 54)
1 lb. carrots, finely chopped
2 celery stalks, finely chopped
4 garlic cloves, minced
1/2 tsp. crushed red pepper
2 T. fresh thyme or 2 tsp. dried thyme
1/4 cup red wine vinegar
Freshly ground pepper
1 lb. pasta shells, cooked al dente

1. Bring Vegetable stock to boil, add all ingredients except pasta shells, and simmer until liquid has been reduced by half.
2. Toss shells into vegetables and serve.

Makes 8 servings.

Each serving contains:
232 calories, 7 gm. protein, 45 gm. carbohydrate, 3 gm. fat, 33 mg. sodium, 50 mg. cholesterol, 3 gm. fiber

ADA Exchange Value
2 Bread, 1/2 Fat, 2 Vegetables
10 % of total calories are from fat

◆ Noodles with Asparagus and Mushrooms ◆

1 lb. wide noodles
1 lb. asparagus, cut diagonally, one inch
1 T. olive oil
1 medium onion, sliced
1 lb. fresh mushrooms
2 T. fresh lemon juice
2 T. chopped fresh basil, or 2 tsp. dried
Black pepper to taste
1/2 cup grated Parmesan cheese

1. Cook noodles al dente and set aside in colander.

2. Blanch asparagus in boiling water for 3 minutes, rinse in cold water.

3. Heat olive oil in skillet and sauté onion. Remove to holding plate. Add mushrooms to skillet, cover for 3 minutes, then uncover and cook until all liquid is absorbed. Return onion to pan. Add lemon juice, basil, and pepper to taste.

4. Refresh noodles with hot water, drain, and add to skillet. Toss together with Parmesan cheese.

Makes 8 servings.

Each serving contains:
282 calories, 12 gm. protein, 44 gm. carbohydrate, 7 gm. fat, 141 mg. sodium, 56 mg. cholesterol, 4 gm. fiber

ADA Exchange Value
2 Bread, 2 Vegetable, 1 Fat
21 % of total calories are from fat

◆ Bow Ties and Broccoli ◆

1 tsp. olive oil
1 shallot, minced
2 red bell peppers, seeded and chopped
1 cup Vegetable Stock (pg. 54)
1 27 1/2-oz. can diced tomatoes
    with juice
1 lb. broccoli florets, blanched in boiling
    water 2 minutes, refreshed under cold
    running water
2 T. chopped fresh basil, or 2 tsp. dried
1 T. chopped fresh oregano, or 1 tsp. dried
1/2 tsp. fresh black pepper
1 lb. bow-tie pasta
1/2 cup fresh grated Parmesan cheese

1. Heat olive oil in large pan. Add shallots and cook 1 minute. Add red peppers and Vegetable Stock and simmer uncovered for 10 minutes.

2. Add tomatoes and simmer 25 minutes. Add basil, oregano, and pepper. Simmer 5 more minutes.

3. While sauce is simmering, cook pasta.

4. Add broccoli to sauce to heat.

5. Toss pasta and sauce together in a large bowl. Sprinkle cheese over top and serve.

Makes 8 servings.

Each serving contains:
262 calories, 11 gm. protein, 45 gm. carbohydrate, 5 gm. fat,
220 mg. sodium, 54 mg. cholesterol, 4 gm. fiber

ADA Exchange Value
2 Bread, 2 Vegetable, 1 Fat
17 % of total calories are from fat

◆ Linguini with Capers, Olives, and Tomatoes ◆

1 medium onion, sliced
2 cloves garlic, minced
2 28-oz. cans diced tomatoes in juice
2 T. capers, drained
2 small cans sliced ripe black olives
1/2 tsp.crushed red pepper
2 tsp. fresh chopped oregano,
   or 1 tsp. dried oregano
1 lb. linguini, cooked al dente
1/4 cup grated Romano cheese

1. In skillet sprayed with nonstick spray, sauté onion and garlic until soft. Add tomatoes, capers, olives, pepper, and oregano. Simmer uncovered for 15 minutes.

2. Toss linguini into sauce and sprinkle with cheese. Serve.

Makes 8 servings.

Each serving contains:
217 calories, 8 gm. protein, 40 gm. carbohydrate, 4 gm. fat,
378 mg. sodium, 3 mg. cholesterol, 4 gm. fiber

ADA Exchange Value
2 Bread, 1 Vegetable , 1 Fat
17 % of total calories are from fat

◆ Kashi Nut Loaf ◆

Serve this with Mushroom Sauce (pg.126) or Basic
Tomato Sauce (pg. 169)

2 1/2 cups cooked Kashi
1 medium onion, chopped
2 stalks celery, chopped
1/2 cup chopped walnuts
1 cup grated low-fat cheese
3/4 cup egg substitute
1/2 tsp. ground pepper

1. Mix all ingredients well in large bowl.
2. Put mixture in a loaf pan that has been sprayed
with nonstick cooking spray. Pack firmly.
3. Bake at 350 degrees for 50 minutes. Let stand
10 minutes before serving.

Makes 6 servings.

Each serving contains:
232 calories, 13 gm. protein, 26 gm. carbohydrate, 9 gm. fat,
168 mg. sodium, 11 mg. cholesterol, 1 gm. fiber

ADA Exchange Value
1 1/2 Bread, 1 Lean Meat, 1 Fat
35 % of total calories are from fat

♦♦♦

Various
Vegetables

♦♦♦

◆ Baked Eggplant ◆

2 medium eggplant, peeled, cut in half,
then cut in thirds
2 cups Vegetable Tomato Sauce (pg. 170)

1. Place the eggplant in a pot of salted water and let
it set for 1/2 hour. Drain and set eggplant on paper
towels.
2. Bring a large pot of water to a boil and blanch
eggplant for 5 minutes.
3. Put eggplant in a baking dish and cover with
Vegetable Tomato Sauce.
4. Bake in a 350-degree oven for 20 minutes.

Makes 6 servings.

Each serving contains:
43 calories, 2 gm. protein, 10 gm. carbohydrate, 1 gm. fat,
423 mg. sodium, 0 cholesterol, 4 gm. fiber

ADA Exchange Value
2 Vegetable
23% of total calories are from fat

◆ Eggplant Parmesan ◆

3 medium eggplant (3 lb.), peeled
   and sliced 1/4-inch thick
1 medium onion, chopped
8 ounces fresh mushrooms
1 28-oz. can whole peeled tomatoes
   in juice
1 14-oz. can Italian tomatoes
2 tsp. Italian seasoning
10 oz. firm tofu
16 oz. nonfat ricotta cheese
1/4 cup grated Parmesan cheese
2 cups part-skim mozzarella cheese

1. Place eggplant on cookie sheets sprayed with
nonstick spray. Lightly spray the top of the eggplant,
bake in 400-degree oven for 10 minutes.

2. Saute onion in skillet sprayed with nonstick
cooking spray. Add mushrooms, cover and cook on
low heat 5 minutes. Uncover, turn heat up, and cook
until all liquid is absorbed.

3. Add tomatoes and 1 tsp. of Italian seasoning.
Simmer uncovered 15 minutes.

4. Place tofu, ricotta, 1 tsp. Italian seasoning, and
Parmesan in food processor. Using steel blade, mix
until well blended.

5. In large baking pan sprayed with nonstick
spray, layer one-half the eggplant. Spoon a light layer of

tomato sauce over this layer, pour the ricotta mixture on and spread evenly. Layer remaining eggplant on top, pouring remaining sauce over. Bake 30 minutes at 350 degrees. 6. Add the mozzarella cheese evenly over top and bake 15 more minutes. Let stand 15 minutes before serving.

Makes 6 servings.

Each serving contains:

341 calories, 27 gm. protein, 25 gm. carbohydrate, 16 gm. fat, 699 mg. sodium, 49 mg. cholesterol, 7 gm. fiber

ADA Exchange Value

4 Vegetable, 3 Medium Fat Meat

43 % of total calories are from fat

◆ Green Beans Amandine ◆

1 lb. fresh green beans, washed and
    trimmed
3 T. "Herbed" Butter Buds (pg. 176)
2 T. slivered almonds, lightly toasted
Fresh ground black pepper

1. Steam green beans until crisp tender. Plunge
into cold water to stop cooking process and to retain
bright green color. Drain well when cooled.

2. Add "Herbed" Butter Buds to a medium-sized
skillet and heat to medium.

3. Add drained green beans. Stir to mix with
Butter Buds. Heat until beans are hot, then quickly stir
in toasted almonds. Serve immediately.

Makes 4 servings. 1 serving = approximately 3/4 cup.

Each serving contains:
53 calories, 2 gm. protein, 8 gm. carbohydrate, 2 gm. fat,
62 mg. sodium, 0 cholesterol, 3 gm. fiber

ADA Exchange Value
2 Vegetable
39% of total calories are from fat

◆ Mushrooms, Chinese Peas ◆ and Water Chestnuts

8 oz. mushrooms, sliced
2 cups Chinese pea pods
1/4 cup sliced water chestnuts

1. Spray a nonstick skillet with nonstick spray. Heat. Add mushrooms. Reduce heat to low. Cover and cook for 3 minutes. Uncover and cook mushrooms until liquid is almost absorbed.
2. Add Chinese pea pods and water chestnuts. Mix well for 30 seconds.
3. Turn off heat, cover, and let stand 2 minutes before serving.

Makes 4 servings.

Each serving contains:
58 calories, 4 gm. protein, 11 gm. carbohydrate, <1 gm. fat, 39 mg. sodium, 0 cholesterol, 4 gm. fiber

ADA Exchange Value
1 Vegetable
<6% of total calories are from fat

◆ Mashed Yellow Squash ◆

1 1/2 lbs. yellow crookneck squash,
   washed and trimmed
1/4 cup "Herbed" Butter Buds (pg. 176)

1. Slice squash into saucepan. Add a small amount of water.

2. Cover and cook on medium high heat approximately 5 to 7 minutes or until squash is tender. Remove from heat. Drain (reserving liquid for Vegetable Stock) and mash with potato masher until slices are moderately broken.

3. Add "Herbed" Butter Buds, mix, and serve.

Makes 3 cups. 1 serving = 1/2 cup

Each serving contains:
19 calories, 1 gm. protein, 4 gm. carbohydrate, 0 fat,
17 mg. sodium, 0 cholesterol, 2 gm. fiber

ADA Exchange Value
1 Vegetable
0% of total calories are from fat

◆ Artichoke Hearts in Wine Sauce ◆

8 to 9 oz. frozen artichoke hearts
1/4 lb. mushrooms, cleaned and quartered
2 tomatoes, peeled and diced
1 tsp. fresh oregano, chopped
1 sprig fresh rosemary, chopped
2 T. flour
1 T. Butter Buds, dry
1/2 cup water or Vegetable Stock
    (pg. 54)
1/4 cup white wine vinegar or Vermouth
Ground black pepper

1. Prepare artichoke hearts according to package directions and drain.

2. Spray nonstick spray into skillet. Sauté mushrooms and add tomatoes, herbs, and artichoke hearts to just heat through.

3. In a small saucepan, mix flour and dry Butter Buds. Gradually add water or stock, stirring to mix and avoid lumps. Add wine.

4. Heat over medium heat until bubbly and thickened. Stir in a few grinds of black pepper.

5. Pour sauce over artichoke mixture and stir to blend. Serve as a side dish or over pasta or rice.

Makes 2 cups. 1 serving = 1/2 cup

Beyond Alfalfa Sprouts & Cheese

Each serving contains:
87 calories, 4 gm. protein, 17 gm. carbohydrate, <1 gm. fat,
113 mg. sodium, 0 cholesterol, 5 gm. fiber

ADA Exchange Value
2 Vegetable
5% of total calories are from fat

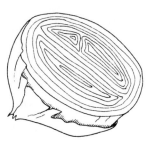

◆ Roasted Onions ◆

2 medium red onions
1/2 cup balsamic vinegar
2 T. fresh oregano or 1 T. dried
Bround black epper

1. Preheat oven to 350 degrees.
2. Skin onions and remove one layer of peel.
3. Slice onion horizontally into 1/2-inch slices.
4. Cover a baking sheet with 1 or 2 layers of foil. Place onion slices on foil. Pour vinegar over onions and sprinkle with oregano.
5. Cover onions with 2 more layers of foil and crimp edges very tight to seal top and bottom layers.
6. Bake in 350-degree oven approximately 1 hour. Onions should be tender and carmelized.

Makes 4 servings.

Each serving contains:
28 calories, 1 gm. protein, 7 gm. carbohydrate, <1 gm. fat,
1 mg. sodium, 0 cholesterol, 1 gm. fiber

ADA Exchange Value
1 Vegetable
0% of total calories are from fat

◆ Chilled Lemon Broccoli ◆

3/4 lb. or about 2 cups broccoli
2 tsp. lemon zest
1/4 cup lemon juice
1 T. olive oil
2 T. water
Ground black pepper
1 tsp. fresh oregano, or 1/2 tsp. dried
2 cloves garlic, crushed
3 T. red bell pepper, diced
3 T. yellow bell pepper, diced

1. Steam broccoli until just crisp tender. Plunge into cold water to stop cooking and bring out green color. Drain.

2. Combine remaining ingredients in food processor and pulse briefly to mix and blend.

3. Pour marinade over broccoli, cover, and refrigerate for several hours.

4. Serve as a side dish, condiment, or appetizer.

Makes 6 1/2-cup servings.

Each serving contains:
43 calories, 2 gm. protein, 5 gm. carbohydrate, 2 gm. fat,
18 mg. sodium. 0 cholesterol, 2 gm. fiber

ADA Exchange Value
1 Vegetable, 1/2 Fat
42% of total calories are from fat

◆ Eleanor's Grated Zucchini ◆

3 medium zucchini, washed and grated
1 T. liquid Butter Buds
1/2 tsp. marjoram
Ground black pepper to taste
1 T. Parmesan cheese

1. Place grated zucchini in medium-sized saucepan. Add Butter Buds and marjoram and heat to medium.
2. Stir frequently until tender, about 4 minutes. Do not overcook.
3. Place in serving dish and sprinkle with ground pepper and Parmesan cheese.

Makes 2 cups. 1 serving = 1/2 cup

Each serving contains:

28 calories, 2 gm. protein, 5 gm. carbohydrate, <1 gm. fat, 42 mg. sodium, 1 mg. cholesterol, 2 gm. fiber

ADA Exchange Value

1 Vegetable
0 calories are from fat

◆ Vegetable Paella ◆

1 medium-sized red onion, peeled and
   sliced
2 cloves garlic, minced
1 cup rice, uncooked*
1 14-oz. can tomatoes
1 cup Vegetable Stock (pg. 54)
1/2 tsp. turmeric
1/2 9-oz. package frozen artichoke hearts
1 red bell pepper cut into strips
1/2 cup frozen small peas
1/4 lb. small whole baby carrots
6 corn cobettes

    1. Spray the bottom of a large, heavy-lidded pot
with nonstick spray. Heat to medium heat and saute
onion rings and garlic.

    2. Add rice and stir to brown lightly. Add Veg-
etable Stock and tomatoes. Stir in turmeric, carrots, and
artichoke hearts. Cover and reduce heat to simmer for
10 minutes.

    3. Add remaining ingredients, cover, and continue
to simmer for 10 to 15 minutes more until rice is done.

*If using brown rice, add carrots and artichoke hearts
when 20 minutes of cooking time remains. Add remaining ingredients 10 minutes later.

◆ ◆ ◆

Makes 6 servings.

Each serving contains:
173 calories, 5 gm. protein, 39 gm. carbohydrate, 1 gm. fat,
177 mg. sodium, 0 cholesterol, 6 gm. fiber

ADA Exchange Value
2 Bread, 1 Vegetable
5% of total calories are from fat

◆ Greens ◆

2 lbs. chard, spinach, mustard greens, or
beet greens

1. Wash greens well.
2. Place in steamer and steam 3 to 5 minutes.

"Greens" are quick and easy to prepare and add a
refreshing variety. "Greens" sometimes have a strong
flavor that many people enjoy. It is a taste that can be
acquired. Serve greens with lemon juice or a mild
vinegar, Herbed Butter Buds (pg. 176), or top with
chopped tomato and onion, and a dollop of Yogurt
Cheese (pg. 177) or nonfat yogurt.

Makes 4 servings.

Each serving contains:
32 calories, 4 gm. protein, 5 gm. carbohydrate, <1 gm. fat,
119 mg. sodium, 0 cholesterol, 6 gm. fiber

ADA Exchange Value
1 Vegetable
<1% of total calories are from fat

◆ Asparagus a la Orange ◆

1 lb. asparagus, cleaned and trimmed
Juice and zest of one orange
2 T. liquid Butter Buds

1. Steam asparagus until just crisp tender. Plunge into cold water to stop cooking process and allow bright green color to appear. Drain.
2. In a skillet, combine orange juice, zest, Butter Buds, and heat.
3. Add asparagus and stir to heat through.

Makes 4 servings.

Each serving contains:
44 calories, 2 gm. protein, 10 gm. carbohydrate, <1 gm. fat,
103 mg. sodium, 0 cholesterol, 2 gm. fiber

ADA Exchange Value
2 Vegetable
0 calories are from fat

◆ Sumptuous Succotash ◆

2 cups frozen lima beans, cooked, reserve
    liquid
2 tsp. fresh rosemary, or 1 tsp. dried
2 tsp. fresh thyme, or 1 tsp. dried
3 cloves garlic, minced
1 onion, chopped
1/2 cup dry red wine
1 14 1/2-oz. can peeled and diced
    tomatoes
Liquid from beans
1 cup corn kernels, fresh or frozen
2 T. fresh parsley, chopped
Fresh ground pepper

1. Spray a large heavy sauce pan with nonstick
spray. Heat to medium high heat and sauté rosemary,
thyme, garlic, and onion for about 2 minutes. Add
wine, tomatoes, lima beans, corn, and about 1/2 cup
bean liquid.
2. Simmer for about 15 minutes, stirring occasionally. Add black pepper.
3. Serve in bowls with parsley sprinkled on top.

Makes 6 servings.

Various Vegetables

Each serving contains:
111 calories, 6 gm. protein, 22 gm. carbohydrate, <1 gm. fat,
237 mg. sodium, 0 cholesterol, 5 gm. fiber

ADA Exchange Value
1 Bread, 1 Vegetable
6% of total calories are from fat

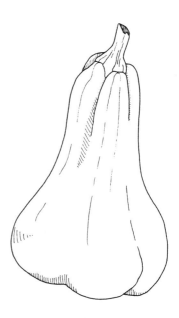

◆ Grilled Mushrooms with Oregano ◆

1/2 lb. mushroom caps, stems removed
Olive oil-flavored nonstick cooking spray
1 tsp. dried oregano leaves

1. Gently wash mushroom caps and pat dry. Put
in a shallow dish and spray with olive oil-flavored
nonstick spray.
2. Heat outdoor or stove-top grill to very hot.
Place mushroom caps on grill upside down and grill 4
to 5 minutes or until slightly tender. Turn caps over and
continue cooking 3 to 5 minutes longer.
3. Remove caps to serving dish and sprinkle with
oregano. Serve.

Makes 4 servings.

Each serving contains:
15 calories, 1 gm. protein, 3 gm. carbohydrate, <1 gm. fat,
3 mg. sodium, 0 cholesterol, 1 gm. fiber

ADA Exchange Value
1 Vegetable
0 calories are from fat

◆ Julienne Carrots and Zucchini ◆

2 tsp. corn oil margarine
2 medium carrots, cut into small strips
2 medium zucchini, cut into small strips
1/2 tsp. dill weed

1. Melt margarine in a skillet. Add zucchini and carrots and toss to cover with margarine.
2. Sprinkle with dill weed and mix well.
3. Turn off heat, cover, and let stand 3 to 5 minutes.

Makes 4 servings.

Each serving contains:
50 calories, 1 gm. protein, 8 gm. carbohydrate, 2 gm. fat,
35 mg. sodium, 0 cholesterol, 3 gm. fiber

ADA Exchange Value
1 1/2 Vegetable
36% of total calories are from fat

◆ Basic Green Beans ◆

2 cups fresh green beans, with stems
    removed, or frozen and thawed
2 tsp. Butter Buds mixed with 1/4 cup
    water
1/2 tsp. minced garlic

1. Steam green beans until tender, about 5 minutes.

2. Heat Butter Buds and water in a medium nonstick skillet. Add garlic and cook lightly.

3. Add green beans and toss until well coated and hot.

Makes 4 servings.

Each serving contains:
22 calories, 1 gm. protein, 5 gm. carbohydrate
<1 gm. fat, 42 mg. sodium, 0 cholesterol, 2 gm. fiber

ADA Exchange Value
1 Vegetable
0 calories are from fat

◆◆◆

Sauces
and More

◆◆◆

◆ Basic Tomato Sauce ◆

This is a basic tomato sauce that I learned from Chef Dimitri Mainos on the Royal Cruise Line. It's a good basic sauce to keep on hand. It makes 8 cups and you can put it in 2-cup containers and freeze so it is ready to use whenever you need it.

> 3 28-oz. cans whole tomatoes with juice
> 6 cloves garlic, diced
> 1 T. olive oil
> 2 tsp. Italian seasoning

1. In a large Dutch oven, place olive oil and sauté garlic until soft.
2. Add whole tomatoes.
3. Using a mortar and pestle, crush Italian seasoning and add to tomato sauce.
4. Simmer over low heat 2 hours, uncovered.
5. Purée sauce in blender or food processor.

Makes 8 cups.

Each cup contains:
58 calories, 2 gm. protein, 9 gm. carbohydrate, 2 gm. fat, 331 mg. sodium, 0 cholesterol, 3 gm. fiber

ADA Exchange Value
2 Vegetable
31% of total calories are from fat

◆ Vegetable Tomato Sauce ◆

1 T. olive oil
1 medium onion, sliced
3 medium carrots, diced
4 stalks celery, sliced
4 cups Basic Tomato Sauce (pg.169)

1. Heat olive oil in a Dutch oven. Add onions and sauté until soft. Add carrots and celery. Sauté until soft.
2. Add Basic Tomato Sauce. Bring to a simmer. Cover and cook for 1/2 hour.
3. Put in blender and purée until smooth.

Makes 6 servings (5 cups).

Each serving contains:
84 calories, 2 gm. protein, 12 gm. carbohydrate, 4 gm. fat,
257 mg. sodium, 0 cholesterol, 4 gm. fiber

ADA Exchange Value
1 Vegetable, 1 Fat
41% of total calories are from fat.

◆ Tomato and Sweet Pepper Sauce ◆

2 shallots, chopped
1 red bell pepper, seeded and chopped
3 14 1/2-oz. cans diced tomatoes in juice
1/4 cup dry vermouth
2 T. fresh chopped tarragon, or 1 tsp. dried
1/2 tsp. cayenne pepper

1. Sauté shallots and pepper in skillet sprayed with nonstick spray. Sauté until tender.
2. Add tomatoes and simmer uncovered 8 to 10 minutes, stirring occasionally.
3. Stir in vermouth and continue simmering until sauce thickens (about 15 minutes).
4. Add tarragon, parsley, and cayenne pepper.

Makes 6 servings.

Each serving contains:
48 calories, 2 gm. protein, 9 gm. carbohydrate, <1 gm. fat,
295 mg. sodium, 0 cholesterol, 3 gm. fiber

ADA Exchange Value
2 Vegetable
0 calories are from fat

◆ Eggplant Tomato Sauce ◆

1 T. olive oil

1 medium onion, chopped

2 medium eggplants, cut in circles, then
  sliced into 1/2-inch sticks

1 lb. mushrooms, quartered

1 28-oz. can diced tomatoes

1 14 1/2-oz. ready-cut tomatoes, Italian
  style

1/2 tsp. black pepper

1. Heat olive oil in Dutch oven and add onions.
Sauté until soft. Add eggplant and mix.

2. In skillet sprayed with nonstick spray, place
mushrooms and cover. Cook over low heat 5 minutes,
remove cover, turn up heat, and sauté until all liquid is
absorbed.

3. Add mushrooms, tomatoes, and pepper to
eggplant. Cover and simmer 1 hour. Uncover and
simmer another hour.

Makes 8 cups.

Each cup contains:
68 calories. 3 gm. protein, 11 gm. carbohydrate, 2 gm. fat,
223 mg. sodium, 0 cholesterol, 4 gm. fiber

ADA Exchange Value
2 Vegetable
26% of total calories are from fat

◆ Broiled Tofu ◆

1/4 cup lemon juice
Zest of one lemon
2 cloves garlic, crushed
1 T. olive oil
1 T. oregano, or 1 1/2 tsp. dried
1 T. basil, or 1 1/2 tsp. dried
10 oz. tofu, drained, pressed, and cut into
1-inch cubes

1. Combine lemon juice, lemon zest, garlic, oil, and herbs in a glass bowl. Add tofu cubes and marinate 8 to 12 hours.
2. Place tofu on thin skewers and broil or cook over hot coals 3 to 5 minutes or until lightly browned.
3. Sprinkle with parsley and serve.

Makes 4 servings.

Each serving contains:
79 calories, 5 gm. protein, 3 gm. carbohydrate, 6 gm. fat,
8 mg. sodium, 0 cholesterol, <1 gm. fiber

ADA Exchange Value
1 Lean Meat
71% of total calories are from fat

◆ Rice Crust ◆

2 cups brown rice, cooked
2 egg whites
2 T. Parmesan cheese

1. Preheat oven to 375 degrees.
2. Combine ingredients in a bowl and mix well.
3. Lightly spray a 9-inch pie plate with nonstick spray. Spoon mixture into a pie plate and pat rice to fit like a pie crust.
4. Bake for 10 to 15 minutes or until very lightly browned.

Use as a basic, fat-free crust for vegetable pies or quiches. 1 serving = 1/8 pie.

Each serving contains:
60 calories, 3 gm. protein, 11 gm. carbohydrate, <1 gm. fat, 36 mg. sodium, 1 mg. cholesterol, 1 gm. fiber

ADA Exchange Value
3/4 Bread
12% of total calories are from fat

◆ Potato Crust ◆

2 medium sized russet potatoes, peeled
and shredded
2 egg whites
1/4 cup Parmesan cheese

1. Preheat oven to 425 degrees.
2. Rinse shredded potatoes in a colander and drain.
Place shreds into a clean dish towel. Fold or wrap towel
around shreds to dry.
3. Place shreds in bowl. Mix in egg whites and
Parmesan cheese.
4. Pat mixture into a pie plate and bake for 20 to
25 minutes or until lightly browned.

Use a a basic crust for quiches, or make into individual
crusts using 4-oz. Pyrex dishes as a mold. Fill with
cooked vegetables.

1 serving = 1/8 pie crust

Each serving contains:
44 calories, 3 gm. protein, 7 gm. carbohydrate, 1 gm. fat,
62 mg. sodium, 2 mg. cholesterol, <1 gm. fiber

ADA Exchange Value
1/2 Bread
20% of total calories are from fat

◆ "Herbed" Butter Buds ◆

1/2 cup liquid Butter Buds - 1 pkt.
1 clove garlic, minced
2 tsp. onion, minced
2 tsp. chives, minced
2 tsp. fresh thyme, minced
2 T. fresh parsley, minced
2 T. fresh basil, minced

Combine all ingredients and allow to mellow for several hours in refrigerator before using.

Makes 3/4 cup. 1 serving = 2 T.

Each serving contains:

33 calories, <1 gm. protein, 8 gm. carbohydrate, 0 fat,
264 mg. sodium, 0 cholesterol, 0 fiber

ADA Exchange Value
Free

◆ Yogurt Cheese ◆

This is an excellent nonfat replacement for cream cheese, mayonnaise, or sour cream. You can make it into a sweet cream or a spicy dip!

16 oz. plain nonfat yogurt, without
added gelatin

1. Place yogurt in a colander lined with coffee filters. Place in a bowl and cover top. Refrigerate for 18 to 24 hours.
2. Throw out liquid and store Yogurt Cheese in a covered container until you are ready to use it.

Makes 8 ounces of cheese.

An 8-ounce serving contains:
225 calories, 24 gm. protein, 32 gm. carbohydrate, negligible fat,
150 sodium, 0 cholesterol, 0 fiber

ADA Exchange Value
2 Nonfat Milk
Negligible fat calories

◆ Crunchy Croutons ◆

Ever wonder what to do with those last few slices of bread in the loaf that somehow become wrinkled, stiff, or dry? Well, as a great money saver and tasty topping maker, these dry bread slices can be converted into Crunchy Croutons in just a few minutes. Store them in your "pantry" in an airtight jar or plastic container with a tight-fitting lid.

2 slices dry whole grain bread
Garlic powder
Basil and oregano to taste

1. Preheat oven to 250 degrees.
2. Cut bread into small cubes and place on a nonstick cookie sheet.
3. Sprinkle lightly with garlic powder, basil, and/or oregano to taste.
4. Bake until lightly browned and crunchy, about 10 to 15 minutes.

Makes 4 servings. 1 serving = 1/4 cup.

Each serving contains:
31 calories, 1 gm. protein, 6 gm. carbohydrate, 4 gm. fat, 79 mg. sodium, 0 cholesterol, 1 gm. fiber

ADA Exchange Value
1/2 Bread

Sweet Treats

◆ Gingerbread ◆

3/4 cup molasses
1/2 cup egg substitute
1 cup low-fat buttermilk
2 1/2 cups unbleached flour (sifted)
1 tsp. Butter Buds, dry
1 tsp. baking soda
1 tsp. cinnamon
2 1/2 tsp. powdered ginger

1. Blend molasses, egg substitute, and buttermilk together.

2. Sift the dry ingredients together and gradually add to liquid ingredients and mix in well.

3. Pour mixture in a Bundt pan and bake in a preheated 350-degree oven for 35 minutes.

Makes 12 aservings.

Each serving contains:
134 calories, 4 gm. protein, 29 gm. carbohydrate, <1 gm. fat,
162 mg. sodium, 1 mg. cholesterol, 0 fiber,

ADA Exchange Value
1 Bread, 1 Fruit
2% of total calories are from fat

◆ Strawberry Tart ◆

2 pints fresh strawberries, washed
   and hulled
4 T. fructose
2 T. cornstarch
1 T. lemon juice
1/4 cup low-calorie strawberry jam
4 oz. Neufchatel cheese
Tart Crust (pg. 183)

1. Prepare Tart Crust, bake and cool.

2. Reserve about 8 whole strawberries. Cut them in half from end to end, sprinkle with 2 T. of fructose and set aside.

3. Mash rest of berries and put in a saucepan with enough cold water to equal 1 1/2 cups. Add cornstarch, 2 T. fructose, and lemon juice. Bring to a low boil and simmer until thickened. Remove from heat and stir in strawberry jam. Cool.

4. Stir Neufchatel cheese and work into spreadable form. Carefully spread on top of cooled tart crust.

5. Place whole berries, bottom side up, around the crust. Pour thickened strawberry mixture over.

6. Chill several hours before serving.

Makes 10 servings.

Each serving contains:

235 calories, 3 gm. protein, 40 gm. carbohydrate, 8 gm. fat,
108 mg. sodium, 9 mg. cholesterol, 3 gm. fiber

ADA Exchange Value
1/2 Bread, 2 Fruit, 2 Fat
31% of total calories are from fat

◆ Tart Crust ◆

1 cup sifted cake flour
2 tsp. fructose
1/4 cup cold corn oil margarine
2 T. ice water

1. Preheat oven to 400 degrees.

2. Combine flour and fructose in a large bowl and cut in margarine with a pastry blender until mixture looks like coarse corn meal. Add just enough water to hold flour mixture together (about 2 T.)

3. Place dough in a 9-inch tart pan and pat it out using your fingers until dough fits into corners and edges. Prick bottom of crust and bake for 10 to 15 minutes or until lightly browned. Cool.

Makes 10 servings.

Each serving contains:
84 calories, 1 gm. protein, 9 gm. carbohydrate. 5 gm. fat, 53 mg. sodium, 0 cholesterol, <1 gm. fiber

ADA Exchange Value
1/2 Bread, 1 Fat
54% of total calories are from fat

◆ Fruit Crisp ◆

4 cups fresh sliced fruit or berries
1/4 cup fructose
Zest of one orange
Juice of one orange
2 T. Butter Buds, liquid
Sprinkle of cinnamon or nutmeg (optional)
1 cup Guiltless Granola (pg. 16)
1 T. oil

1. Preheat oven to 375 degrees.
2. In a medium-sized heat-proof casserole, combine and lightly toss all ingredients except granola and oil.
3. Mix granola with oil in a small bowl and sprinkle mixture on top of fruit.
4. Bake for 30 minutes.

Makes 6 servings.

Each serving contains:
155 calories, 3 gm. protein, 27 gm. carbohydrate, 5 gm. fat,
25 mg. sodium, 0 cholesterol, 3 gm. fiber

ADA Exchange Value
2 Fruit, 1 Fat
29% of total calories are from fat

◆ Soft Tofu Smoothie ◆

10 oz. soft tofu
1 cup fresh or frozen fruit (frozen preferred)
1 tsp. vanilla (optional)
1/4 tsp. cinnamon (optional)
1/8 tsp. nutmeg (optional)

Blend all ingredients until smooth and creamy.

Makes 2 servings.

Each serving contains:
118 calories, 10 gm. protein, 8 gm. carbohydrate, 6 gm. fat,
9 mg. sodium, 0 cholesterol, 2 gm. fiber

ADA Exchange Value
1 Lean Meat, 1/2 Fruit, 1/2 Fat
44% of total calories are from fat

◆ Banana Date Tofu Smoothie ◆

10 oz. soft tofu
2 dates, pitted
1/2 banana, frozen
1/4 cup apple juice

Place all ingredients in a blender and blend until smooth.

Makes 2 servings.

Each serving contains:
178 calories, 10 gm. protein, 25 gm. carbohydrate, 6 gm. fat,
12 mg. sodium, 0 cholesterol, 2 gm. fiber

ADA Exchange Value
1 Lean Meat, 1 1/2 Fruit
28% of total calories are from fat

◆ Raspberry Pudding Cheesecake ◆

2 1/4 cups unbleached flour, sifted
1 1/2 tsp. baking powder
1/2 tsp. baking soda
1/2 cup fructose
2 tsp. vanilla
1/2 cup egg substitute
2 cups nonfat cottage cheese, whipped
1/2 cup low-fat buttermilk
3 T. Wax Orchards Raspberry Fanciful*

1. Sift flour, baking powder, and baking soda together.
2. Blend fructose, vanilla, egg substitute, cottage cheese, and buttermilk together.
3. Gradually add flour mixture to cottage cheese mixture.
4. Spray a tube pan with nonstick spray. Spoon Raspberry Fanciful evenly around pan. Spoon cake mixture in pan and bake 45 minutes in oven preheated to 350 degrees.

*You can use any sugar-free jam.

Makes 10 servings.

Each serving contains:
158 calories, 9 gm. protein, 29 gm. carbohydrate, <1 gm. fat, 173 mg. sodium, 3 mg. cholesterol, 0 fiber

ADA Exchange Value
1 Bread, 1 Fruit, 1 Lean Meat
<5% of total calories are from fat

◆ Chocolate Cheesecake ◆

Crust

1 1/4 cups graham cracker crumbs
2 T. Wax Orchard Classic Fudge Sweet

1. Put graham crackers and Fudge Sweet in food processor and process until well mixed.
2. Press mixture in a 9-inch pie pan.

Filling

3 cups low-fat cottage cheese
1/3 cup fructose
1/4 cup imported cocoa powder
1 tsp. vanilla
1 T. Wax Orchards Classic Fudge Sweet
2 tsp. cornstarch

1. Put cottage cheese in food processor and whip until smooth.
2. Put remaining ingredients in the food processor and blend well.
3. Pour mixture in the graham cracker crust and bake at 350 degrees for 20 minutes.

Makes 8 servings.

Sweet Treats

Each serving contains:
171 calories, 11 gm. protein, 25 gm. carbohydrate, 3 gm. fat,
134 mg. sodium, 6 mg. cholesterol, 0.5 gm. fiber

ADA Exchange Value
1/2 Bread, 1 Fruit, 1 Lean Meat, 1/2 Fat
16% of total calories are from fat

◆ Chocolate Pudding Cake ◆

1 cup fructose
1/2 cup cocoa
1/2 cup egg substitute
1 cup low-fat buttermilk
5 oz. baby food prunes
1 tsp. baking soda
2 cups all purpose flour

1. Mix fructose, cocoa, egg substitute, buttermilk, and prunes together.
2. Slowly add baking soda and flour. Mix well.
3. Pour into 9-inch tube or molded cake pan.
4. Bake at 350 degrees for 35 minutes.

Makes 12 servings.

Each serving contains:
149 calories, 4 gm. protein, 31 gm. carbohydrate, 1 gm. fat,
158 mg. sodium, 2 mg. cholesterol, 1 gm. fiber

ADA Exchange Value
2 Bread
6% of total calories are from fat

◆ Chocolate Mocha Cheesecake ◆

2 1/2 cups unbleached flour, sifted
1 1/2 tsp. baking powder
1/2 tsp. baking soda
3/4 cup imported cocoa powder
2 tsp. instant coffee powder
1 cup fructose
2 tsp. vanilla
1 cup egg substitute
3 cups nonfat cottage cheese, whipped
1/2 cup 1% milk

1. Sift flour, baking powder, baking soda, instant coffee, and cocoa powder together.

2. In another bowl, blend fructose, vanilla, egg substitute, cottage cheese and milk together.

3. Gradually add flour mixture to cottage cheese mixture.

4. Spray a large tube pan with nonstick spray. Spoon cake mixture into pan and bake 45 minutes in oven preheated to 350 degrees.

Serves 10.

Each serving contains:
223 calories, 15 gm. protein, 39 gm. carbohydrate, 1 gm. fat, 204 mg. sodium, 4 mg. cholesterol, 4 gm. fiber

ADA Exchange Value
1 Bread, 1 Fruit, 1 1/2 Lean Meat
4% of total calories are from fat

✦ Pumpkin Pie with Graham Cracker Crust ✦

Crust

1 cup graham cracker crumbs
2 T. fructose
1/2 tsp. allspice
2 T. corn oil margarine, melted

Mix all ingredients together. Press into a 9-inch pie pan. Bake in a preheated oven at 375 degrees for 8 minutes. Cool.

Filling

4 egg whites, slightly beaten
1 1/2 cups solid packed canned pumpkin
1/2 cup fructose
1 tsp. ground cinnamon
1/2 tsp. ground ginger
1/4 tsp. ground cloves
1 1/2 cups 1% milk

1. Preheat oven to 425 degrees.
2. Mix all ingredients together and pour into crust.
3. Bake 15 minutes, then reduce heat to 350 degrees and bake 45 minutes or until knife inserted in the center of pie comes out clean. Cool before serving.

✦ ✦ ✦

Makes 8 servings.

Each serving contains:

189 calories, 5 gm. protein, 30 gm. carbohydrate, 6 gm. fat,
156 mg. sodium, 4 mg. cholesterol, 1 gm. fiber

ADA Exchange Value

1 Bread, 1 Fruit, 1 Fat
29% of calories are from fat.

◆ Pumpkin Cake ◆

This recipe will make 2 large Bundt cakes or 4 small ones.

Mix together:

8 oz. egg substitute

1 cup brown sugar

1/2 cup sugar

1 tsp. vanilla

1 cup nonfat milk

1 29-oz. can pumpkin

Mix together:

2 cups all-purpose flour

2 cups oatmeal

1 T. baking soda

1 tsp. baking powder

3 T. pumpkin pie spice

2 cups chopped walnuts

1 cup raisins

1. Fold dry ingredients into other mixture until mixed well.

2. Pour mixture into pans sprayed with nonstick spray.

3. Bake in preheated oven at 350 degrees for 1 hour.

4. Let cool, unmold on plate, sprinkle with powdered sugar.

◆ ◆ ◆

Sweet Treats

Each recipe makes 24 servings.

Each serving contains:
194 calories, 6 gm. protein, 30 gm. carbohydrate, 7 gm. fat,
178 mg. sodium, 0.2 mg. cholesterol, 2 gm. fiber

ADA Exchange Value
2 Bread, 1 Fat
32% of calories are from fat

◆ Brownies ◆

3 egg whites
1/3 cup nonfat milk
1 tsp. vanilla
1 cup unsweetened applesauce
1/2 cup fructose (or 2/3 cup sugar)
1 cup imported cocoa powder
1 cup mini semisweet chocholate chips
1/2 cup chopped walnuts

1. Mix together egg whites, nonfat milk, vanilla, fructose, and apple sauce.

2. Sift flour, baking powder, and cocoa powder into liquid mixture and mix well.

3. Fold in chocolate chips and walnuts.

4. Pour into an 8" pan sprayed with nonstick spray.

5. Bake in preheated 350-degree oven for 45 minutes.

6. Cool and cut into 16 bars.

Makes 16 servings.

Each serving contains:
165 calories, 3 gm. protein, 27 gm. carbohydrate, 6 gm. fat,
41 mg. sodium, 1 gm. fiber

ADA Exchange Values
1 1/2 Bread, 1 Fat
33% of calories are from fat

◆ Lemon Cake ◆

8 oz. egg substitute
1/2 cup fructose
3/4 cup nonfat yogurt
1 tsp. vanilla
2 T. lemon juice*
2 T. lemon rind*
1 cup presifted self-rising flour
1 cup presifted unbleached flour

1. Preheat oven to 325 degrees.
2. Mix egg substitute, fructose, nonfat yogurt, vanilla, lemon juice and rind together.
3. Fold in flours.
4. Put mixture in a loaf or Bundt pan.
5. Bake 45 minutes.

Serves 12

Each serving contains:
143 calories, 5 gm. protein, 0 fat, 50 mg. sodium

ADA Exchange Value
2 Bread
0 calories from fat

* 2 T. orange juice concentrate and 2 T. orange rind can be substituted for Orange Cake.

◆ Index ◆

Index

203

Index

CHRONIMED Publishing Books of Related Interest

The Healthy Eater's Guide to Family & Chain Restaurants by Hope S. Warshaw, M.M.Sc., R.D. Here's the only guide that tells you how to eat healthier in over 100 of America's most popular family and chain restaurants. It offers complete and up-to-date nutrition information and suggests which items to choose and avoid.

004214,   ISBN 1-56561-017-2 $9.95

The Label Reader's Pocket Dictionary of Food Additives by J. Michael Lapchick with Cindy Appleseth, R.Ph., is the only quick-reference guide to more than 250 of today's most common food additives– found in virtually everything we eat. It has the latest findings in an easy-to-read dictionary format with all the information you'll need to make intelligent food decisions.

004224,   ISBN 1-56561-027-X $4.95

One Year of Healthy, Hearty, and Quick One-Dish Meals by Pam Spaude and Jan Owan-McMenamin, R.D., is a collection of 365 easy-to-make healthy and tasty family favorites and unique creations that are meals in themselves. Most of the dishes take under 30 minutes to prepare.

004217,   ISBN 1-56561-019-9 $12.95

Let Them Eat Cake by Virginia N. White with Rosa A. Mo, R.D. If you're looking for delicious and healthy pies, cookies, puddings, and cakes, this book will give you your just desserts. With easy, step-by-step instructions, this innovative cookbook features complete nutrition information, the latest exchange values, and tips on making your favorite snacks more healthful.

004206,   ISBN 1-56561-011-3 $12.95

Beyone Alfalfa Sprouts and Cheese: The Healthy Meatless Cookbook by Judy Gilliard and Joy Kirkpatrick, R.D., includes creative and savory meatless dishes using ingredients found in just about every grocery store. It also contains helpful cooking tips, complete nutrition information, and the latest exchange values.

004218,   ISBN 1-56561-020-2 $12.95

All-American Low-Fat Meals in Minutes by M.J. Smith, M.A., R.D., L.D. Filled with tantalizing recipes and valuable tips, this cookbook makes great-tasting low-fat foods a snap for holidays, special occasions, or everyday. Most recipes take only minutes to prepare.

004079,   ISBN 0-937721-73-5 $12.95

The Guiltless Gourmet by Judy Gilliard and Joy Kirkpatrick, R.D. A perfect fusion of sound nutrition and creative cooking, this book is loaded with delicious recipes high in flavor and low in fat, sugar, calories, cholesterol, and salt.

004021,   ISBN 0-937721-23-9 $9.95

The Guiltless Gourmet Goes Ethnic by Judy Gilliard and Joy Kirkpatrick, R.D. More than a cookbook, this sequel to *The Guiltless Gourmet* shows how easy it is to lower the sugar, calories, sodium, and fat in your favorite ethnic dishes—without sacrificing taste.

004072, ISBN 0-937721-68-9 $11.95

European Cuisine from the Guiltless Gourmet by Judy Gilliard and Joy Kirkpatrick, R.D. This book shows you how to lower the sugar, salt, cholesterol, total fat, and calories in delicious Greek, English, German, Russian, and Scandinavian dishes. Plus it features complete nutrition information and the latest exchange values.

004085, ISBN 0-937721-81-6 $11.95

The Joy of Snacks by Nancy Cooper, R.D. Offers more than 200 delicious recipes and nutrition information for hearty snacks, including sandwiches, appetizers, soups, spreads, cookies, muffins, and treats especially for kids. The book also suggests guidelines for selecting convenience snacks and interpreting information on food labels.

004086, ISBN 0-937721-82-4 $12.95

Convenience Food Facts by Arlene Monk, R.D., C.D.E with Marion Franz, R.D., M.S. Includes complete nutrition information, tips, and exchange values on more than 1,500 popular name-brand processed foods commonly found in grocery store freezers and shelves. Helps you plan easy-to-prepare, nutritious meals.

004081, ISBN 0-937721-77-8 $10.95

Fast Food Facts by Marion Franz, R.D., M.S. This revised and up-to-date bestseller shows how to make smart nutrition choices at fast food restaurants—and tells what to avoid. Includes complete nutrition information on more than 1,000 menu offerings from the 21 largest fast food chains.

Standard-size edition 004068, ISBN 0-937721-67-0 $6.95
Pocket edition 004073, ISBN 0-937721-69-7 $4.95

Exchanges for All Occasions by Marion Franz, R.D., M.S. Exchanges and meal planning suggestions for just about any occasion, sample meal plans, special tips for people with diabetes, and more.

004003, ISBN 0-937721-22-0 $12.95

Fight Fat & Win by Elaine Moquette-Magee, R.D., M.P.H. This breakthrough book explains how to easily incorporate low-fat dietary guidelines into every modern eating experience, from fast-food and common restaurants to quick meals at home, simply by making smarter choices.

004070, ISBN 0-937721-65-4 $9.95

Pass the Pepper Please by Diane Reader, R.D., and Marion Franz, R.D., M.S. This imaginative book is loaded with fresh and clear suggestions for cutting back on salt to lower blood pressure and maintain good health.

004020, ISBN 0-937721-17-4 $3.95